ART & LOVE

An Illustrated Anthology of Love Poetry

ART & LOVE

An Illustrated Anthology of Love Poetry

Selected and Introduced by KATE FARRELL

The Metropolitan Museum of Art · New York

A Bulfinch Press Book / Little, Brown and Company
Boston · Toronto · London

FRONT COVER: *Still Life: Flowers and Fruit* (detail).
Severin Roesen, German, active in America 1848–72.
Oil on canvas, between 1850 and 1855.

BACK COVER: *The Proposal.*
Adolphe William Bouguereau, French, 1825–1905.
Oil on canvas, 1872.

PAGE 13: *Rubens, His Wife Helena Fourment, and Their Son Peter Paul.*
Peter Paul Rubens, Flemish, 1577–1640.
Oil on wood, ca. 1639.

PAGE 29: *In the Meadow.*
Pierre Auguste Renoir, French, 1841–1919.
Oil on canvas.

PAGE 45: *The Love Letter.*
Jean Honoré Fragonard, French, 1732–1806.
Oil on canvas.

PAGE 67: *Terrace at Sainte-Adresse.*
Claude Monet, French, 1840–1926.
Oil on canvas.

PAGE 85: *Sulking.*
Edgar Degas, French, 1834–1917.
Oil on canvas, ca. 1869–71.

PAGE 103: *Venus and Adonis.*
Titian (Tiziano Vecellio), Italian (Venetian), ca. 1488–1576.
Oil on canvas.

PAGE 123: *Two Members of the Gozzadini Family.*
Italian (Emilian), 15th century.
Tempera on panel.

PAGE 143: *Nasturtiums and the "Dance," II.*
Henri Matisse, French, 1869–1954.
Oil on canvas, 1912.

This book owes much to the patience, enthusiasm, and intelligence of Mary Beth Brewer, my editor in the Department of Special Publications. Thanks also to Elizabeth Stoneman, who ably shepherded the book through production.   KF

For acknowledgments of the use of copyrighted material, see page 162.

First Edition

LIBRARY OF CONGRESS
CATALOGING-IN-PUBLICATION DATA

Art & love : an illustrated anthology of love poetry / selected and introduced by Kate Farrell.—1st ed.
    p.   cm.
    ISBN 0-87099-576-6 (MMA).—ISBN 0-8212-1771-2 (Bulfinch Press—distributor)
    1. Love poetry.   2. Love in art.   I. Farrell, Kate.
II. Metropolitan Museum of Art (New York, N.Y.)   III. Title: Art and love.
PN6110.L6A66   1990   90-31791
808.81′9354—dc20   CIP

PUBLISHED BY
The Metropolitan Museum of Art and Bulfinch Press
    Bulfinch Press is an imprint and trademark of Little, Brown and Company (Inc.)
    Published simultaneously in Canada
    by Little, Brown & Company (Canada) Limited
Produced by the Department of Special Publications, The Metropolitan Museum of Art
Designed by Peter Oldenburg
Photography by The Metropolitan Museum of Art Photograph Studio
Printed and bound in Italy by A. Mondadori, Verona

CONTENTS

Go, Lovely Rose

Let Me Count the Ways

The Marriage of True Minds

Give All to Love

INTRODUCTION

"At the touch of love, everyone becomes a poet," wrote Plato almost 2,400 years ago, summing up the natural affinity between love and poetry and alluding to the power of both: Love can turn ordinary people into poets, and poetry can help people clarify love's many mysteries. A book of love poetry illustrated with works from the splendid collections of The Metropolitan Museum of Art seems a perfect way to show what a great inspiration love, through the ages, has been to the arts. It is a chance to show, too, how eloquently poetry and the other arts reflect the important part that love plays in our lives.

In putting this book together, I chose the poems first and then found works of art that seemed to illuminate them in some way. Given limited space and limitless possibilities, I picked poems that I liked and thought others would like, poems that looked at many sides of love and showed poetry's wonderful diversity. There is poetry from many times and places; light- and heavy-hearted poems; old favorites and surprises; poems with all sorts of moods, outlooks, and styles.

The connection between a poem and a work of art is more often imaginative than literal. The mysterious force that animates Henri Matisse's *Icarus* resembles that which flows through Raymond Carver's poem "Energy." Claude Monet's misty, self-reflective *Poplars* accentuates the mood of tender longing in the poems by Federico García Lorca and James Laughlin that appear alongside it. At times, it seemed fitting to pair a poem from one culture with a work of art from a very different one. Anne Bradstreet's 17th-century poem to her husband, for example, found its match in a statue of the Egyptian Memisabu and his wife, who lived more than 4,000 years ago.

The poems fell naturally into eight sections. The title of each section is taken from the poem that introduces it. There are poems about familial love (*My-ness*); friendship (*Oath of Friendship*); the quest for romantic love (*Go, Lovely Rose*); and poems that praise the beloved's beauty, inner and outer (*Let Me Count the Ways*). Other poems speak of troubled love (*The Mess of Love*) and of lost love and parting (*Yesterday He Still Looked in My Eyes*). Naturally, many of the poems celebrate the harmony of mature love (*The Marriage of True Minds*), and the final section contains poems about love as an idea and ideal (*Give All to Love*).

This collection is a small bouquet gathered from a vast, richly varied garden, one that belongs to us all. The arts challenge and console us, lift our standards and deepen our thinking, enliven our days and inspire our lives. I hope this book encourages further exploration of the garden.

Kate Farrell

My-ness

MY-NESS

"My parents, my husband, my brother, my sister."
I am listening in a cafeteria at breakfast.
The women's voices rustle, fulfill themselves
In a ritual no doubt necessary.
I glance sidelong at their moving lips
And I delight in being here on earth
For one more moment, with them, here on earth,
To celebrate our tiny, tiny my-ness.

CZESLAW MILOSZ, Polish, b. 1911

For the Little One. William Merritt Chase, American, 1849–1916. Oil on canvas, ca. 1895.

MY BABY HAS NO NAME YET

My baby has no name yet;
like a new-born chick or a puppy,
my baby is not named yet.

What numberless texts I examined
at dawn and night and evening over again!
But not one character did I find
which is as lovely as the child.

Starry field of the sky,
or heap of pearls in the depth.
Where can the name be found, how can I?

My baby has no name yet;
like an unnamed bluebird or white flowers
from the farthest land for the first,
I have no name for this baby of ours.

KIM NAM-JO, Korean, b. 1927

The Abraham Pixler Family. American, ca. 1815. Ink and watercolor on paper.

SEVENTEEN MONTHS

This girl child speaks five words.
No for no and no for yes, "no" for either
   no or yes.
"Teewee" for wheat or oats or corn or barley
   or any food taken with a spoon.
"Go way" as an edict to keep your distance
   and let her determinations operate.

"Spoon" for spoon or cup or anything to be
   handled, all instruments, tools, paraphernalia of
   utility and convenience are SPOONS.
Mama is her only epithet and synonym for God and
   the Government and the one force of majesty
   and intelligence obeying the call of pity, hunger,
   pain, cold, dark—MAMA, MAMA, MAMA.

      CARL SANDBURG, American, 1878–1967

ROCKING MY CHILD

The sea its millions of waves
   is rocking, divine,
hearing the loving seas,
   I'm rocking my child.

The wandering wind in the night
   is rocking the fields of wheat,
hearing the loving winds,
   I'm rocking my child.

God the father his thousands of worlds
   is rocking without a sound.
Feeling his hand in the shadows,
   I'm rocking my child.

      GABRIELA MISTRAL, Chilean, 1889–1957

Midnight: Mother and Sleepy Child. Kitagawa Utamaro,
Japanese, 1753–1806. Woodblock print in colors from
Customs of Women in the Twelve Hours, 1790.

CHILDREN

My nephew, who is six years old, is called
    "Tortoise";
My daughter of three—little "Summer Dress."
One is beginning to learn to joke and talk;
The other can already recite poems and songs.
At morning they play clinging about my feet;
At night they sleep pillowed against my dress.

Why, children, did you reach the world so late,
Coming to me just when my years are spent?
Young things draw our feelings to them;
Old people easily give their hearts.
The sweetest vintage at last turns sour;
The full moon in the end begins to wane.
And so with men the bonds of love and affection
Soon may change to a load of sorrow and care.
But all the world is bound by love's ties;
Why did I think that I alone should escape?

      Po Chü-i, Chinese, 772–846

The Lacemaker (detail). Nicolaes Maes, Dutch
(1634–1693). Oil on canvas.

First Steps. Vincent van Gogh, Dutch, 1853–1890. Oil on canvas, 1890.

A CHILD IS SOMETHING ELSE AGAIN

A child is something else again. Wakes up
in the afternoon and in an instant he's full
    of words,
in an instant he's humming, in an instant warm,
instant light, instant darkness.

A child is Job. They've already placed their
    bets on him
but he doesn't know it. He scratches his body
for pleasure. Nothing hurts yet.
They're training him to be a polite Job,
to say "Thank you" when the Lord has given,
to say "You're welcome" when the Lord has
    taken away.

A child is vengeance.
A child is a missile into the coming generations.
I launched him: I'm still trembling.

A child is something else again: on a rainy
    spring day
glimpsing the Garden of Eden through the
    fence,
kissing him in his sleep,
hearing footsteps in the wet pine needles.
A child delivers you from death.
Child, Garden, Rain, Fate.

YEHUDA AMICHAI, Israeli, b. 1924

INFANCY

My father got on his horse and went to the
    field.
My mother stayed sitting and sewing.
My little brother slept.
A small boy alone under the mango trees,
I read the story of Robinson Crusoe,
the long story that never comes to an end.

At noon, white with light, a voice that had
    learned
lullabies long ago in the slave-quarters
    —and never forgot—
called us for coffee.
Coffee blacker than the black old woman
delicious coffee
good coffee.

My mother stayed sitting and sewing
watching me:
Shh—don't wake the boy.
She stopped the cradle when a mosquito
    had lit
and gave a sigh . . . how deep!
Away off there my father went riding
through the farm's endless wastes.

And I didn't know that my story
was prettier than that of Robinson Crusoe.

CARLOS DRUMMOND DE ANDRADE, Brazilian, b. 1902

OUR CHILD

Oh child, do you know, do you know
where you come from?

From a lake
with white and hungry sea gulls.

Hummingbird and Passionflowers (detail).
Martin Johnson Heade, American, 1819–1904.
Oil on canvas.

Besides the wintry water
she and I built
a red bonfire
wearing away our lips
from kissing each other's souls,
throwing everything into the fire,
burning up our life.

This is the way you arrived in the world.

But in order to see me
and in order to see you one day
she crossed over the seas
and in order to embrace
her small waist
I walked the whole earth,
with wars and mountains,
with sand and spines.

This is the way you arrived in the world.

From so many places you come,
from the water and from the earth,
from the fire and from the snow,
from so far away you walk
toward the two of us,
from the terrible love
that has enchained us,
so we want to know
what you are like, what you say to us,
because you know more
about the world than we gave you.

Like a great storm
the two of us shake

the tree of life
down to the most hidden
fibers of its roots
and you appear now,
singing in the leaves,
on the highest branch
we reached with you.

PABLO NERUDA, Chilean, 1904–1973

FOR THEE, LITTLE BOY

FROM ECLOGUE 4

For thee, little boy, will the earth pour forth gifts
All untilled, give thee gifts
First the wandering ivy and foxglove
Then colocasia and the laughing acanthus
Uncalled the goats will come home with their milk
No longer need the herds fear the lion
Thy cradle itself will bloom with sweet flowers

The serpent will die
The poison plant will wither
Assyrian herbs will spring up everywhere

And when thou art old enough to read of heroes
And of thy father's great deeds
Old enough to understand the meaning of courage
Then will the plain grow yellow with ripe grain
Grapes will grow on brambles
Hard old oaks drip honey.

VIRGIL, Roman, 70–19 B.C.

Don Manuel Osorio Manrique de Zuñiga (1784–1792).
Francisco Goya, Spanish, 1746–1828. Oil on canvas.

[21]

FOR AITANA

(9th of August, 1956)

Aitana, my child, Springtime bows
to give you fifteen small and delicate flowers.
You are still fashioned from air, and all your
    things
still seem charmed by a fragile light.

Aitana, my child, how I wish I could make
the fairest winds blow forever for you,
and that I could comb more lights and
    smooth out more roses
on your young wings of messenger breeze.

Aitana, my child, since you are air and are
like air and you soar off on the wind when
    you wish,
happy, hushed and blind and alone in your bliss,

though I'd open new skies to your wings,
don't forget that even the air can lose its leaves
    in a flash,
the air, dear child Aitana, Aitana, my child.

RAFAEL ALBERTI, Spanish, b. 1902

Spring. Detail of an embroidered hanging. French,
ca. 1683. Silk, wool, and silver thread on canvas.

HOME-SICKNESS

Of College I am tired; I wish to be at home,
Far from the pompous tutor's voice, and the hated
   school-boy's groan.

I wish that I had freedom to walk about at will;
That I no more was troubled by my Greek and
   slate and quill.

I wish to see my kitten, to hear my ape rejoice,
To listen to my nightingale's or parrot's lovely voice.

And England does not suit me: it's cold and full of
   snow;
So different from black Africa's warm, sunny,
   genial glow.

I'm shivering in the day-time, and shivering all
   the night:
I'm called poor, startled, withered wretch, and
   miserable wight!

And oh! I miss my brother, I miss his gentle smile
Which used so many long dark hours of sorrow to
   beguile.

I miss my dearest mother; I now no longer find
Aught half so mild as she was,—so careful and so
   kind.

Oh, I have not my father's, my noble father's arms
To guard me from all wickedness, and keep me
   safe from harms.

I hear his voice no longer; I see no more his eye
Smile on me in my misery: to whom now shall I fly?

CHARLOTTE BRONTË, English, 1816–1855

Soap Bubbles. Thomas Couture, French, 1815–1879.
Oil on canvas.

TO MY SISTER

It is the first mild day of March:
Each minute sweeter than before,
The redbreast sings from the tall larch
That stands beside our door.

There is a blessing in the air,
Which seems a sense of joy to yield,
To the bare trees, and mountains bare,
And grass in the green field.

My sister! ('tis a wish of mine)
Now that our morning meal is done,
Make haste, your morning task resign;
Come forth and feel the sun.

Edward will come with you;—and, pray,
Put on with speed your woodland dress;
And bring no book: for this one day
We'll give to idleness.

No joyless forms shall regulate
Our living calendar:
We from to-day, my Friend, will date
The opening of the year.

Love, now a universal birth,
From heart to heart is stealing,
From earth to man, from man to earth:
—It is the hour of feeling.

One moment now may give us more
Than years of toiling reason:
Our minds shall drink at every pore
The spirit of the season.

Some silent laws our heart will make,
Which they shall long obey:
We for the year to come may take
Our temper from to-day.

And from the blessed power that rolls
About, below, above,
We'll frame the measure of our souls:
They shall be tuned to love.

Then come, my Sister! come, I pray,
With speed put on your woodland dress;
And bring no book: for this one day
We'll give to idleness.

WILLIAM WORDSWORTH, English, 1770–1850

The Flowering Orchard.
Vincent van Gogh, Dutch,
1853–1890. Oil on canvas, 1888.

Interior with Figure Sewing.
Edouard Vuillard, French,
1868–1940. Oil on panel, 1896.

IN MEMORY OF MY MOTHER

You will have the road gate open, the front
    door ajar
The kettle boiling and a table set
By the window looking out at the sycamores—
And your loving heart lying in wait

For me coming up among the poplar trees.
You'll know my breathing and my walk
And it will be a summer evening on those roads
Lonely with leaves of thought.

We will be choked with the grief of things growing,
The silence of dark-green air
Life too rich—the nettles, docks and thistles
All answering the prodigal's prayer.

You will know I am coming though I send no word
For you were lover who could tell
A man's thoughts—my thoughts—though I hid them—
Through you I knew Woman and did not fear her
    spell.

PATRICK KAVANAGH, Irish, 1904–1967

A CELEBRATION FOR
GEORGE SARTON

I never saw my father old;
I never saw my father cold.
His stride, staccato vital,
His talk struck from pure metal
Simple as gold, and all his learning
Only to light a passion's burning.
So, beaming like a lesser god,
He bounced upon the earth he trod,
And people marveled on the street
At this stout man's impetuous feet.

Loved donkeys, children, awkward ducks,
Loved to retell old simple jokes;
Lived in a world of innocence
Where loneliness could be intense;
Wrote letters until very late,
Found comfort in an orange cat—
Rufus and George exchanged no word,
But while George worked his Rufus purred,
And neighbors looked up at his light,
Warmed by the scholar working late.

I never saw my father passive;
He was electrically massive.
He never hurried, so he said,
And yet a fire burned in his head;
He worked as poets work, for love,
And gathered in a world alive,
While black and white above his door
Spoke Mystery, the avatar—
An Arabic inscription flowed
Like singing: "In the name of God."

And when he died, he died so swift
His death was like a final gift.
He went out when the ride was full,
Still undiminished, bountiful;
The scholar and the gentle soul.
The passion and the life were whole.
And now death's wake is only praise,
As when a neighbor writes and says:
"I did not know your father, but
His light was there. I miss the light."

MAY SARTON, American, b. 1912

**Portrait of a Man, Probably Lucas van Uffele
(1583?–1637)**. Anthony van Dyck, Flemish, 1599–1641.
Oil on canvas.

ENERGY

Last night at my daughter's, near Blaine,
she did her best to tell me
what went wrong
between her mother and me.

"Energy. You two's energy was all wrong."
She looks like her mother
when her mother was young.
Laughs like her.
Moves the drift of hair
from her forehead, like her mother.
Can take a cigarette down
to the filter in three draws,
just like her mother. I thought
this visit would be easy. Wrong.
This is hard, brother. Those years
spilling over into my sleep when I try
to sleep. To wake to find a thousand
cigarettes in the ashtray and every
light in the house burning. I can't
pretend to understand anything:
today I'll be carried
three thousand miles away into
the loving arms of another woman, not
her mother. No. She's caught
in the flywheel of a new love.
I turn off the last light
and close the door.
Moving toward whatever ancient thing
it is that works the chains
and pulls us so relentlessly on.

RAYMOND CARVER, American, 1938–1988

Icarus. Henri Matisse, French, 1869–1954. Pochoir from *Jazz*, published by Tériade, Paris, 1947.

*Oath of
Friendship*

OATH OF FRIENDSHIP

Shang ya!
I want to be your friend
For ever and ever without break or decay.
When the hills are all flat
And the rivers are all dry,
When it lightens and thunders in winter,
When it rains and snows in summer,
When Heaven and Earth mingle—
Not till then will I part from you.

ANONYMOUS, China, 1st century B.C.

NONE OF US ARE AS YOUNG

None of us are as young
as we were. So what?
Friendship never ages.

W. H. AUDEN, American (b. England), 1907–1973

SONNET

Guido, I wish that you and Lapo and I
Were carried off by magic
And put in a boat, which, every time there was wind,
Would sail on the ocean exactly where we wanted.

In this way storms and other dangerous weather
Wouldn't be able to harm us—
And I wish that, since we all were of one mind,
We would want more and more to be together.

And I wish that Vanna and Lagia too
And the girl whose name on the list is number
    thirty
Were put in the boat by the magician too

And that we all did nothing but talk about love
And I wish that they were just as glad to be there
As I believe the three of us would be.

DANTE ALIGHIERI, Italian, 1265–1321

Fantastic Landscape. Francesco Guardi, Italian (Venetian), 1712–1793. Oil on canvas.

Boy Blowing Bubbles. Jean Baptiste Siméon Chardin, French, 1699–1779. Oil on canvas.

YOU PLAYMATES OF MINE

You playmates of mine in the scattered parks of
     the city,
small friends from a childhood of long ago:
how we found and liked one another, hesitantly,
and, like the lamb with the talking scroll,

spoke with our silence. When we were filled with
     joy
it belonged to no one: it was simply there.
And how it dissolved among all the adults who
     passed by
and in the fears of the endless year.

Wheels rolled past us, we stood and stared at the
     carriages;
houses surrounded us, solid but untrue—and
     none
of them ever knew us. *What* in that world was
     real?

Nothing. Only the balls. Their magnificent arches.
Not even the children . . . But sometimes one,
oh a vanishing one, stepped under the plummeting
     ball.

(In memoriam Egon von Rilke)

RAINER MARIA RILKE, Austrian, 1875–1926

[32]

THE THOUSANDTH MAN

One man in a thousand, Solomon says,
Will stick more close than a brother.
And it's worth while seeking him half your days
If you find him before the other.
Nine hundred and ninety-nine depend
On what the world sees in you,
But the Thousandth Man will stand your friend
With the whole round world agin you.

'Tis neither promise nor prayer nor show
Will settle the finding for 'ee.
Nine hundred and ninety-nine of 'em go
By your looks, or your acts, or your glory.
But if he finds you and you find him,
The rest of the world don't matter;
For the Thousandth Man will sink or swim
With you in any water.

You can use his purse with no more talk
Than he uses yours for his spendings,
And laugh and meet in your daily walk
As though there had been no lendings.
Nine hundred and ninety-nine of them call
For silver and gold in their dealings;
But the Thousandth Man he's worth 'em all,
Because you can show him your feelings.

His wrong's your wrong, and his right's your right,
In season or out of season.
Stand up and back it in all men's sight—
With *that* for your only reason!
Nine hundred and ninety-nine can't bide
The shame or mocking or laughter,
But the Thousandth Man will stand by your side
To the gallows-foot—and after!

RUDYARD KIPLING, English, 1865–1936

The Studio. Winslow Homer, American, 1836–1910.
Oil on canvas, 1867.

AT THE END OF SPRING

To Yüan Chên (A.D. 810)

The flower of the pear-tree gathers and turns to
   fruit;
The swallows' eggs have hatched into young birds.
When the Seasons' changes thus confront the mind
What comfort can the Doctrine of Tao give?
It will teach me to watch the days and months fly
Without grieving that Youth slips away;

If the Fleeting World is but a long dream,
It does not matter whether one is young or old.
But ever since the day that my friend left my side
And has lived an exile in the City of Chiang-ling,
There is one wish I cannot quite destroy:
That from time to time we may chance to meet
   again.

Po CHÜ-I, Chinese, 772–846

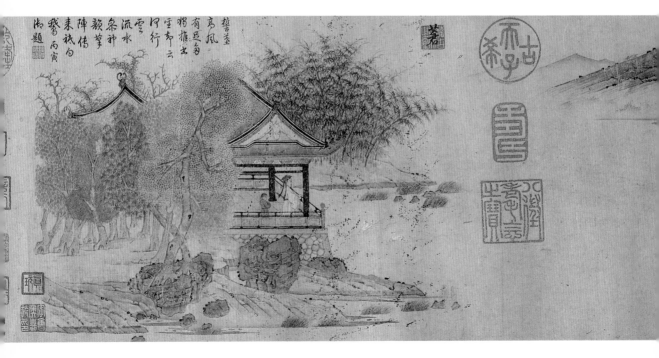

HEARING THAT HIS FRIEND WAS COMING BACK FROM THE WAR

In old days those who went to fight
In three years had one year's leave.
But in *this* war the soldiers are never changed;
They must go on fighting till they die on the
    battlefield.
I thought of you, so weak and indolent,
Hopelessly trying to learn to march and drill.
That a young man should ever come home again
Seemed about as likely as that the sky should fall.
Since I got the news that you were coming back,
Twice I have mounted to the high wall of your
    home.
I found your brother mending your horse's stall;
I found your mother sewing your new clothes.
I am half afraid; perhaps it is not true;
Yet I never weary of watching for you on the road.
Each day I go out at the City Gate
With a flask of wine, lest you should come thirsty.
Oh that I could shrink the surface of the World,
So that suddenly I might find you standing at my
    side!

WANG CHIEN, Chinese, 756–835

Wang Hsi-chih Watching Geese. Ch'ien Hsüan, Chinese, ca. 1235–after 1301. Handscroll in ink, color, and gold on paper.

SONNET XXX

When to the sessions of sweet silent thought,
I summon up remembrance of things past,
I sigh the lack of many a thing I sought,
And with old woes new wail my dear time's waste:
Then can I drown an eye (unus'd to flow)
For precious friends hid in death's dateless night,
And weep afresh love's long-since cancell'd woe,
And moan th' expense of many a vanish'd sight:
Then can I grieve at grievances foregone,
And heavily from woe to woe tell o'er
The sad account of fore-bemoaned moan,
Which I new pay as if not paid before.
    But if the while I think on thee (dear friend)
    All losses are restor'd, and sorrows end.

WILLIAM SHAKESPEARE, English, 1564–1616

Dr. Emanuel Lasker and His Brother. Frank Eugene, American, 1865–1936. Platinum print, 1907.

BARS

I love bars and taverns
beside the sea,
where people talk and drink
just to drink and talk.
Where Joe Nobody comes in and asks for
his drink straight,
and there are Joe Brawl and Joe Blade
and Joe Blow and even Simple Joe,
just plain old Joe.

There white waves
break in friendship;
a friendship of the people, without rhetoric,
a wave of "hello!" and "how are you doing?"
There it smells of fish,
of mangrove, of rum, of salt
and of a sweaty shirt put in the sun to dry.

Look me up, brother, and you'll find me
(in Havana, in Oporto,
in Jacmel, in Shanghai)
with plain folk
who just to drink and talk
people the bars and taverns
beside the sea.

NICOLÁS GUILLÉN, Cuban, b. 1902

The Smokers. Adriaen Brouwer, Flemish, 1606(?)–1638. Oil on wood, ca. 1636.

AFTER DRINKING ALL NIGHT WITH A FRIEND, WE GO OUT IN A BOAT AT DAWN TO SEE WHO CAN WRITE THE BEST POEM

These pines, these fall oaks, these rocks,
This water dark and touched by wind—
I am like you, you dark boat,
Drifting over water fed by cool springs.

Beneath the waters, since I was a boy,
I have dreamt of strange and dark treasures,
Not of gold, or strange stones, but the true
Gift, beneath the pale lakes of Minnesota.

This morning also, drifting in the dawn wind,
I sense my hands, and my shoes, and this ink—
Drifting, as all of this body drifts,
Above the clouds of the flesh and the stone.

A few friendships, a few dawns, a few glimpses
    of grass,
A few oars weathered by the snow and the heat,
So we drift toward shore, over cold waters,
No longer caring if we drift or go straight.

ROBERT BLY, American, b. 1926

[38]

Lake George. John Frederick Kensett, American, 1816–1872. Oil on canvas, 1869.

THE TELEPHONE

"When I was just as far as I could walk
From here today,
There was an hour
All still
When leaning my head against a flower
I heard you talk.
Don't say I didn't, for I heard you say—
You spoke from that flower on the windowsill—
Do you remember what it was you said?"

"First tell me what it was you thought you heard."

"Having found the flower and driven a bee away,
I leaned my head,
And holding by the stalk,
I listened and I thought I caught the word—
What was it? Did you call me by my name?
Or did you say—
Someone said 'Come'—I heard it as I bowed."

"I may have thought as much, but not aloud."

"Well, so I came."

ROBERT FROST, American, 1874–1963

Mount Fuji and Flowers. David Hockney, British, b. 1937. Acrylic on canvas, 1972.

LETTER TO N.Y.

For Louise Crane

In your next letter I wish you'd say
where you are going and what you are doing;
how are the plays, and after the plays
what other pleasures you're pursuing:

taking cabs in the middle of the night,
driving as if to save your soul
where the road goes round and round the park
and the meter glares like a moral owl,

and the trees look so queer and green
standing alone in big black caves
and suddenly you're in a different place
where everything seems to happen in waves,

and most of the jokes you just can't catch,
like dirty words rubbed off a slate,
and the songs are loud but somehow dim
and it gets so terribly late,

and coming out of the brownstone house
to the gray sidewalk, the watered street,
one side of the buildings rises with the sun
like a glistening field of wheat.

—Wheat, not oats, dear. I'm afraid
if it's wheat it's none of your sowing,
nevertheless I'd like to know
what you are doing and where you are going.

ELIZABETH BISHOP, American, 1911–1979

TO L. R-M

There are certain ladies in our land
Still living and still unafraid
Whose hearts have known a lot of pain,
Whose eyes have shed so many tears,
Who welcomed pity with disdain
And view the fast encroaching years
Humorously and undismayed.

There are certain ladies in our land,
Whose courage is too deeply bred
To merit unreflecting praise.
For them no easy, glib escape;
No mystic hopes confuse their days;
They can identify the shape
Of what's to come, devoid of dread.

There are certain ladies in our land
Who bring to Life the gift of gay
Uncompromising sanity.
The past, for them, is safe and sure.
Perhaps their only vanity
Is that they know they can endure
The rigours of another day.

NOEL COWARD, English, 1899–1973

The Lafayette. John Sloan, American, 1871–1951.
Oil on canvas, 1927.

POEM

Here we are again together
as the buds burst over the trees their
light cries, walking around a pond in yellow weather.

Fresh clouds, and further
oh I do not care to go!
not beyond this circling friendship,
damp new air and fluttering snow
remaining long enough to make the leaves
excessive in the quickness of their mild return,
not needing more than earth and friends to see the winter so.

FRANK O'HARA, American, 1926–1966

THE NORTH COAST

Those picnics covered with sand
No money made them more gay
We passed over hills in the night
And walked along beaches by day.

Sage in the rain, or the sand
Spattered by new-falling rain.
That ocean was too cold to swim
But we did it again and again.

GARY SNYDER, American, b. 1930

On the Beach at Trouville. Eugène Boudin, French, 1824–1898. Oil on wood, 1863.

AUTUMN LEAVES

Mountains and mountains and mountains
rolling, rolling, rolling:
all overgrown with trees, trees, trees,
turning, turning, turning:
but in the field where we are
strolling, strolling, strolling,
the leaves on trees
are green, green, green.
"Soon," I say, "these leaves,
the ginkgo, the willow and the beech,
will all be
turning, turning, turning.
That smouldering red off there
is a swamp maple."

Then we come to a fence
where one who has given
his life to poetry leans.
Next to him a sign proclaims,
ETERNAL HAPPINESS. Am I
dreaming about Frank again?
Frank among the leaves
all turning, turning, turning.

JAMES SCHUYLER, American, b. 1923

PARTING

For me who go,
     for you who stay—
          two autumns.

TANIGUCHI BUSON, Japanese, 1716–1783

Cypresses. Vincent van Gogh, Dutch, 1853–1890. Oil on canvas.

The Oxbow. Thomas Cole, American, 1801–1848.
Oil on canvas, 1836.

THE MEETING OF THE WATERS

There is not in the wide world a valley so sweet
As that vale in whose bosom the bright waters
    meet;
Oh! the last rays of feeling and life must depart,
Ere the bloom of that valley shall fade from my
    heart.

Yet it *was* not that Nature had shed o'er the scene
Her purest of crystal and brightest of green;
'Twas *not* her soft magic of streamlet or hill,
Oh! no,—it was something more exquisite still.

'Twas that friends, the belov'd of my bosom, were
    near,
Who made every dear scene of enchantment more
    dear,
And who felt how the best charms of nature
    improve,
When we see them reflected from looks that we
    love.

Sweet vale of Avoca! how calm could I rest
In thy bosom of shade, with the friends I love
    best,
Where the storms that we feel in this cold world
    should cease,
And our hearts, like thy waters, be mingled in
    peace.

THOMAS MOORE, Irish, 1779–1852

Go,
Lovely
Rose

SONG

Go, lovely rose—
Tell her that wastes her time and me,
That now she knows,
When I resemble her to thee,
How sweet and fair she seems to be.

Tell her that's young,
And shuns to have her graces spied,
That hadst thou sprung
In deserts where no men abide,
Thou must have uncommended died.

Small is the worth
Of beauty from the light retired:
Bid her come forth,
Suffer herself to be desired,
And not blush so to be admired.

Then die!—that she
The common fate of all things rare
May read in thee;
How small a part of time they share
That are so wondrous sweet and fair!

EDMUND WALLER, English, 1606–1687

Allegorical Figure. Detail of an armoire. French (Burgundian School), late 16th century. Walnut, carved, painted, and gilded.

The Storm. Pierre Auguste Cot, French, 1837–1883. Oil on canvas, 1880.

TO HIS LOVE

Come away, come, sweet love,
The golden morning breaks,
All the earth, all the air
Of love and pleasure speaks,
Teach thine arms then to embrace,
And sweet rosy lips to kiss,
And mix our souls in mutual bliss.
Eyes were made for beauty's grace,
Viewing, rueing love's long pain,
Procur'd by beauty's rude disdain.

Come away, come, sweet love,
The golden morning wastes,
While the sun from his sphere
His fiery arrows casts:
Making all the shadows fly,
Playing, staying in the grove,
To entertain the stealth of love,
Thither, sweet love, let us hie,
Flying, dying, in desire,
Wing'd with sweet hopes and heav'nly fire.

Come away, come, sweet love,
Do not in vain adorn
Beauty's grace that should rise
Like to the naked morn:
Lilies on the river's side,
And fair Cyprian flowers new blown,
Desire no beauties but their own,

Ornament is nurse of pride,
Pleasure, measure, love's delight,
Haste then, sweet love, our wished flight.

ANONYMOUS, ENGLISH

Landscape. Needlework upholstery on the back of an easy chair. American (Newport, Rhode Island), 1758.

I HID MY LOVE

I hid my love when young till I
Couldn't bear the buzzing of a fly;
I hid my love to my despite
Till I could not bear to look at light:
I dare not gaze upon her face
But left her memory in each place;
Where'er I saw a wild flower lie
I kissed and bade my love good-bye.

I met her in the greenest dells,
Where dewdrops pearl the wood bluebells;
The lost breeze kissed her bright blue eye,
The bee kissed and went singing by,
A sunbeam found a passage there,
A gold chain round her neck so fair;
As secret as the wild bee's song
She lay there all the summer long.

I hid my love in field and town
Till e'en the breeze would knock me down;
The bees seemed singing ballads o'er,
The fly's bass turned a lion's roar;
And even silence found a tongue,
To haunt me all the summer long;
The riddle nature could not prove
Was nothing else but secret love.

JOHN CLARE, English, 1793–1864

SONG

"Oh! Love," they said, "is King of Kings,
    And Triumph is his crown.
Earth fades in flame before his wings,
    And Sun and Moon bow down."—
But that, I knew, would never do;
    And Heaven is all too high.
So whenever I met a Queen, I said,
    I will not catch her eye.

"Oh! Love," they said, and "Love," they said,
    "The gift of Love is this;
A crown of thorns about thy head,
    And vinegar to thy kiss!"—
But Tragedy is not for me;
    And I'm content to be gay.
So whenever I spied a Tragic Lady,
    I went another way.

And so I never feared to see
    You wander down the street,
Or come across the fields to me
    On ordinary feet.
For what they'd never told me of,
    And what I never knew;
It was that all the time, my love,
    Love would be merely you.

RUPERT BROOKE, English, 1887–1915

The Proposal. Adolphe William Bouguereau, French,
1825–1905. Oil on canvas, 1872.

THE UNKNOWN

She is most fair,
And when they see her pass
The poets' ladies
Look no more in the glass
But after her.

Pygmalion and Galatea. Jean Léon Gérôme, French, 1824–1904. Oil on canvas, ca. 1890.

On a bleak moor
Running under the moon
She lures a poet,
Once proud or happy, soon
Far from his door.

Beside a train,
Because they saw her go,
Or failed to see her,
Travellers and watchers know
Another pain.

The simple lack
Of her is more to me
Than others' presence,
Whether life splendid be
Or utter black.

I have not seen,
I have no news of her;
I can tell only
She is not here, but there
She might have been.

She is to be kissed
Only perhaps by me;
She may be seeking
Me and no other; she
May not exist.

EDWARD THOMAS, English, 1878–1917

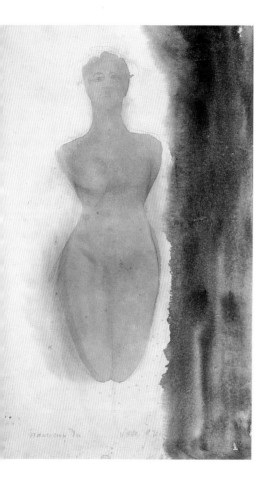

YOU WHO NEVER ARRIVED

You who never arrived
in my arms, Beloved, who were lost
from the start,
I don't even know what songs
would please you. I have given up trying
to recognize you in the surging wave of the next
moment. All the immense
images in me—the far-off, deeply-felt landscape,
cities, towers, and bridges, and un-
suspected turns in the path,
and those powerful lands that were once
pulsing with the life of the gods—
all rise within me to mean
you, who forever elude me.

You, Beloved, who are all
the gardens I have ever gazed at,
longing. An open window
in a country house—, and you almost
stepped out, pensive, to meet me. Streets that I chanced upon,—
you had just walked down them and vanished.
And sometimes, in a shop, the mirrors
were still dizzy with your presence and, startled, gave back
my too-sudden image. Who knows? perhaps the same
bird echoed through both of us
yesterday, separate, in the evening . . .

RAINER MARIA RILKE, Austrian, 1875–1926

Origin of the Greek Vase. Auguste Rodin, French,
1840–1917. Watercolor, gouache, and pencil.

LOVE SONG

I lie here thinking of you:—

the stain of love
is upon the world!
Yellow, yellow, yellow
it eats into the leaves,
smears with saffron
the horned branches that lean
heavily
against a smooth purple sky!
There is no light
only a honey-thick stain
that drips from leaf to leaf
and limb to limb
spoiling the colors
of the whole world—

you far off there under
the wine-red selvage of the west!

WILLIAM CARLOS WILLIAMS, American,
1883–1963

IF YOU WERE COMING
IN THE FALL

If you were coming in the fall,
I'd brush the summer by
With half a smile and half a spurn,
As housewives do a fly.

If I could see you in a year,
I'd wind the months in balls,
And put them each in separate drawers,
Until their time befalls.

If only centuries delayed,
I'd count them on my hand,
Subtracting till my fingers dropped
Into Van Diemen's land.

If certain, when this life was out,
That yours and mine should be,
I'd toss it yonder like a rind,
And taste eternity.

But now, all ignorant of the length
Of time's uncertain wing,
It goads me, like the goblin bee,
That will not state its sting.

EMILY DICKINSON, American, 1830–1886

Autumn River. Wolf Kahn, American, b. 1927.
Oil on canvas, 1979.

I HAVE LOVED HOURS AT SEA

I have loved hours at sea, gray cities,
    The fragile secret of a flower,
Music, the making of a poem
    That gave me heaven for an hour;

First stars above a snowy hill,
    Voices of people kindly and wise,
And the great look of love, long hidden,
    Found at last in meeting eyes.

        SARA TEASDALE, American, 1884–1933.

Portrait of a Man and a Woman at a Casement.
Fra Filippo Lippi, Italian (Florentine), ca. 1406–1469.
Tempera on wood.

TO HIS COY MISTRESS

Had we but world enough, and time,
This coyness, Lady, were no crime.
We would sit down and think which way
To walk and pass our long love's day.
Thou by the Indian Ganges' side
Shouldst rubies find: I by the tide
Of Humber would complain. I would
Love you ten years before the Flood,
And you should, if you please, refuse
Till the conversion of the Jews.
My vegetable love should grow
Vaster than empires, and more slow;
An hundred years should go to praise
Thine eyes and on thy forehead gaze;
Two hundred to adore each breast;
But thirty thousand to the rest;
An age at least to every part,
And the last age should show your heart;
For, Lady, you deserve this state,
Nor would I love at lower rate.

    But at my back I always hear
Time's winged chariot hurrying near;
And yonder all before us lie
Deserts of vast eternity.
Thy beauty shall no more be found,
Nor, in thy marble vault, shall sound
My echoing song: then worms shall try
That long preserved virginity,
And your quaint honour turn to dust,
And into ashes all my lust:
The grave's a fine and private place,
But none, I think, do there embrace.
    Now therefore, while the youthful hue
Sits on thy skin like morning dew,
And while thy willing soul transpires
At every pore with instant fires,
Now let us sport us while we may,
And now, like amorous birds of prey,
Rather at once our time devour
Than languish in his slow-chapt power.
Let us roll all our strength and all
Our sweetness up into one ball,
And tear our pleasures with rough strife
Thorough the iron gates of life:
Thus, though we cannot make our sun
Stand still, yet we will make him run.

ANDREW MARVELL, English, 1621–1678

The Stolen Kiss. Jean Honoré Fragonard, French,
1732–1806. Oil on canvas.

LOVE'S PHILOSOPHY

The fountains mingle with the river
    And the rivers with the Ocean,
The winds of Heaven mix for ever
    With a sweet emotion;
Nothing in the world is single;
    All things by a law divine
In one spirit meet and mingle,
    Why not I with thine?—

See the mountains kiss high Heaven
    And the waves clasp one another;
No sister-flower would be forgiven
    If it disdained its brother;
And the sunlight clasps the earth
    And the moonbeams kiss the sea:
What is all this sweet work worth
    If thou kiss not me?

      PERCY BYSSHE SHELLEY, English, 1792–1822

The Interrupted Sleep (detail). François Boucher, French, 1703–1770. Oil on canvas, 1750.

THE KISS

"I saw you take his kiss!" " 'Tis true."
    "O, modesty!" " 'Twas strictly kept:
He thought me asleep; at least I knew
    He thought I thought he thought I slept."

    COVENTRY PATMORE, English, 1823–1896

The Garden of the Tuileries on a Winter Afternoon, I (detail). Camille Pissarro, French, 1830–1903. Oil on canvas.

[56]

THE GARDEN

Of the thousands and thousands of years
Time would take to prepare
They would not suffice
To entice
That small second of eternity
When you kissed me
When I kissed you
One morning in the light of winter
In Parc Montsouris in Paris
In Paris
On earth
Earth that is a star.

Jacques Prévert, French, 1900–1977

RECIPE FOR HAPPINESS
KHABAROVSK OR ANYPLACE

One grand boulevard with trees
with one grand café in sun
with strong black coffee in very small cups

One not necessarily very beautiful
man or woman who loves you

One fine day

Lawrence Ferlinghetti, American, b. 1920

THE PASSIONATE SHEPHERD TO HIS LOVE

Come live with me and be my love,
And we will all the pleasures prove
That valleys, groves, hills, and fields,
Woods, or steepy mountain yields.

And we will sit upon the rocks,
Seeing the shepherds feed their flocks,
By shallow rivers to whose falls
Melodious birds sing madrigals.

And I will make thee beds of roses
And a thousand fragrant posies,
A cap of flowers, and a kirtle
Embroidered all with leaves of myrtle;

A gown made of the finest wool
Which from our pretty lambs we pull;
Fair lined slippers for the cold,
With buckles of the purest gold;

A belt of straw and ivy buds,
With coral clasps and amber studs:
And if these pleasures may thee move,
Come live with me, and be my love.

The shepherds' swains shall dance and sing
For thy delight each May morning:
If these delights thy mind may move,
Then live with me and be my love.

CHRISTOPHER MARLOWE, English, 1564–1593

Embroidered Cabinet. Box (top on right) decorated with scenes representing the five senses. English, ca. 1650–75. White satin, with seed-pearls and coral.

THE NYMPH'S REPLY TO THE SHEPHERD

If all the world and love were young,
And truth in every shepherd's tongue,
These pretty pleasures might me move
To live with thee and be thy love.

Time drives the flocks from field to fold
When rivers rage and rocks grow cold,
And Philomel becometh dumb;
The rest complains of cares to come.

The flowers do fade, and wanton fields
To wayward winter reckoning yields;
A honey tongue, a heart of gall,
Is fancy's spring, but sorrow's fall.

Thy gowns, thy shoes, thy beds of roses,
Thy cap, thy kirtle, and thy posies
Soon break, soon wither, soon forgotten—
In folly ripe, in reason rotten.

Thy belt of straw and ivy buds,
Thy coral clasps and amber studs,
All these in me no means can move
To come to thee and be thy love.

But could youth last and love still breed,
Had joys no date nor age no need,
Then these delights my mind might move
To live with thee and be thy love.

SIR WALTER RALEGH, English, ca. 1552–1618

GRAY ROOM

Although you sit in a room that is gray,
Except for the silver
Of the straw-paper,
And pick
At your pale white gown;
Or lift one of the green beads
Of your necklace,
To let it fall;
Or gaze at your green fan
Printed with the red branches of a red willow;
Or, with one finger,
Move the leaf in the bowl—
The leaf that has fallen from the branches of the
    forsythia
Beside you . . .
What is all this?
I know how furiously your heart is beating.

WALLACE STEVENS, American, 1879-1955

Jallais Hill, Pontoise. Camille Pissarro, French, 1830–1903. Oil on canvas, 1867.

EVERYTHING PROMISED HIM TO ME

Everything promised him to me:
the fading amber edge of the sky,
and the sweet dreams of Christmas,
and the wind at Easter, loud with bells,

and the red shoots of the grapevine,
and waterfalls in the park,
and two large dragonflies
on the rusty iron fencepost.

And I could only believe
that he would be mine
as I walked along the high slopes,
the path of burning stones.

ANNA AKHMATOVA, Russian, 1889–1966

HE WISHES FOR THE CLOTHS OF HEAVEN

Had I the heavens' embroidered cloths,
Enwrought with golden and silver light,
The blue and the dim and the dark cloths
Of night and light and the half-light,
I would spread the cloths under your feet:
But I, being poor, have only my dreams;
I have spread my dreams under your feet;
Tread softly because you tread on my dreams.

WILLIAM BUTLER YEATS, Irish, 1865–1939

Across the Room (detail). Edmund C. Tarbell, American, 1862–1938. Oil on canvas, ca. 1899.

SONNET

How shall I work that she may not forget
The wretch to whom her beauty most belongs?
Like an old fisherman, I'll knot a net
Patiently squatting, bending songs to songs.
Like an old fisherman, I'll spread a mesh
Well-stretched and wide, but strengthy to
   constrain
From last escape the lively, flapping flesh
Of the soft carp, her heart, causing no pain.

Well must that heart go darting here and there
Meet this and that, and beat for him and him,
And seeming to despise my circling snare.
Glittering in sunshine, grey in shadow, swim,
   Lurk, frolic, double, dive, head out to sea—
   Ay, but not free, thou Lovely One, not free!

OWEN BARFIELD, English, b. 1898

The Rapids of Kajikazawa. Katsushika Hokusai,
Japanese, 1760–1849. Woodblock print in colors from
The Thirty-six Views of Fuji, 1823–29.

JULIET

How did the party go in Portman Square?
I cannot tell you; Juliet was not there.
And how did Lady Gaster's party go?
Juliet was next me and I do not know.

Hilaire Belloc, English, 1870–1953

THE OLYMPIC GIRL

The sort of girl I like to see
Smiles down from her great height at me.
She stands in strong, athletic pose
And wrinkles her *retroussé* nose.
Is it distaste that makes her frown,
So furious and freckled, down
On an unhealthy worm like me?
Or am I what she likes to see?
I do not know, though much I care.
εἴθε γενοίμην . . . would I were
(Forgive me, shade of Rupert Brooke)
An object fit to claim her look.
Oh! would I were her racket press'd
With hard excitement to her breast
And swished into the sunlit air
Arm-high above her tousled hair,
And banged against the bounding ball
"Oh! Plung!" my tauten'd strings would call,
"Oh! Plung! my darling, break my strings

For you I will do brilliant things."
And when the match is over, I
Would flop beside you, hear you sigh;
And then, with what supreme caress,
You'd tuck me up into my press.
Fair tigress of the tennis courts,
So short in sleeve and strong in shorts,
Little, alas, to you I mean,
For I am bald and old and green.

Sir John Betjeman, English, 1906–1984

Tennis at Newport. George Bellows, American, 1882–1925.
Oil on canvas, 1919.

The Heart, South of Naples. Jim Dine, American, b. 1935. Oil on canvas, 1986.

Pair of Dancers. Modeled by Joseph Nees, German (Ludwigsburg), active 1754–1773. Hard-paste porcelain, 1760–63.

PERSONAL COLUMN

. . . As to my heart, that may as well be forgotten
or labelled: Owner will dispose of same
to a good home, refs. exchgd., h.&c.,
previous experience desired but not essential
or let on a short lease to suit convenience.

BASIL BUNTING, English, 1900–1985

IS IT A MONTH

Is it a month since I and you
In the starlight of Glen Dubh
Stretched beneath a hazel bough
Kissed from ear and throat to brow,
Since your fingers, neck, and chin
Made the bars that fenced me in,
Till Paradise seemed but a wreck
Near your bosom, brow, and neck
And stars grew wilder, growing wise,
In the splendour of your eyes!
Since the weasel wandered near
Whilst we kissed from ear to ear
And the wet and withered leaves
Blew about your cap and sleeves,
Till the moon sank tired through the ledge
Of the wet and windy hedge?
And we took the starry lane
Back to Dublin town again.

JOHN SYNGE, Irish, 1871–1909

O BLUSH NOT SO! O BLUSH NOT SO!

O blush not so! O blush not so!
    Or I shall think you knowing;
And if you smile, the blushing while,
    Then maidenheads are going.

There's a blush for won't, and a blush for shan't,
    And a blush for having done it;
There's a blush for thought, and a blush
  for nought,
    And a blush for just begun it.

O sigh not so! O sigh not so!
    For it sounds of Eve's sweet pippin;
By those loosen'd hips, you have tasted the pips,
    And fought in an amorous nipping.

Will you play once more, at nice cut-core,
    For it only will last our youth out;
And we have the prime of the kissing time,
    We have not one sweet tooth out.

There's a sigh for yes, and a sigh for no,
    And a sigh for I can't bear it!
O what can be done? Shall we stay or run?
    O cut the sweet apple and share it!

JOHN KEATS, English, 1795–1821

[65]

COME, AND BE MY BABY

The highway is full of big cars
going nowhere fast
And folks is smoking anything that'll burn
Some people wrap their lives around a cocktail
    glass
And you sit wondering
where you're going to turn
I got it.
Come. And be my baby.

Some prophets say the world is gonna end
    tomorrow
But others say we've got a week or two
The paper is full of every kind of blooming
    horror
And you sit wondering
What you're gonna do.
I got it.
Come. And be my baby.

MAYA ANGELOU, American, b. 1928

The Block. Romare Bearden, American, 1914–1988. Cut
and pasted paper on Masonite, three of six panels, 1971.

Let Me Count the Ways

SONNET XLIII, FROM THE PORTUGUESE

How do I love thee? Let me count the ways.
I love thee to the depth and breadth and height
My soul can reach, when feeling out of sight
For the ends of Being and ideal Grace.
I love thee to the level of everyday's
Most quiet need, by sun and candle-light.
I love thee freely, as men strive for Right;
I love thee purely, as they turn from Praise.
I love thee with the passion put to use
In my old griefs, and with my childhood's faith.
I love thee with a love I seemed to lose
With my lost saints!—I love thee with the breath,
Smiles, tears, of all my life!—and, if God choose,
I shall but love thee better after death.

ELIZABETH BARRETT BROWNING, English,
1806–1861

The Music Lesson. Modeled by Joseph Willems.
English (Chelsea). Soft-paste porcelain, 1762–1765.

MADRIGAL

My Love in her attire doth show her wit,
   It doth so well become her;
For every season she hath dressings fit,
   For Winter, Spring, and Summer.
     No beauty she doth miss
       When all her robes are on:
     But Beauty's self she is
       When all her robes are gone.

ANONYMOUS, English, 17th century

THE TWO USES

The eye is not more exquisitely designed
For seeing than it is for being loved.
The same lips curved to speak are curved to kiss.
Even the workaday and practical arm
Becomes all love for love's sake to the lover.

If this is nature's thrift, love thrives on it.
Love never asks the body different
Or ever wants it less ambiguous,
The eye being lovelier for what it sees,
The arm for all it does, the lips for speaking.

ROBERT FRANCIS, American, b. 1901

The Toilet of Venus. François Boucher, French,
1703–1770. Oil on canvas, 1751.

[69]

TO LAURA

I saw the tracks of angels in the earth,
The beauty of heaven walking by itself on the
    world.
Joke or sorrow now, it seems a dream
Shadow, or smoke.

I saw a kind of rain that made the sun ashamed,
And heard her, speaking sad words, make
    mountains
Shift, the rivers stop.

Love, wisdom, valor, pity, pain,
Made better harmony with weeping
Than any other likely to be heard in the world.

And the air and the wind were so filled with this
    deep music
No single leaf moved on its still branch.

          PETRARCH, Italian, 1304–1374

The Lake of Zug. Joseph Mallord William Turner, English, 1775–1851. Watercolor, gouache, and colored chalk, 1843.

EVE SPEAKS TO ADAM

FROM PARADISE LOST

With thee conversing I forget all time,
All seasons and their change, all please alike.
Sweet is the breath of morn, her rising sweet,
With charm of earliest birds; pleasant the sun
When first on this delightful land he spreads
His orient beams, on herb, tree, fruit, and flower,
Glistring with dew; fragrant the fertile earth
After soft showers; and sweet the coming on
Of grateful evening mild, then silent night
With this her solemn bird and this fair moon,
And these the gems of heav'n, her starry train:
But neither breath of morn when she ascends
With charm of earliest birds, nor rising sun
On this delightful land, nor herb, fruit, flower,
Glistring with dew, nor fragrance after showers,
Nor grateful evening mild, nor silent night
With this her solemn bird, nor walk by moon,
Or glittering starlight without thee is sweet.

JOHN MILTON, English, 1608–1674

The Creation of Eve: "And She Shall Be Called Woman." William Blake, English, 1757–1827. Pen and black ink and watercolor.

[71]

ONE DAY I WROTE HER NAME UPON THE STRAND

One day I wrote her name upon the strand,
 But came the waves and washed it away:
 Again I wrote it with a second hand,
 But came the tide, and made my pains his prey.
Vain man, said she, that dost in vain assay
 A mortal thing so to immortalize,
 For I myself shall like to this decay,
 And eke my name be wiped out likewise.

Not so, (quod I) let baser things devise
 To die in dust, but you shall live by fame:
 My verse your virtues rare shall eternize,
 And in the heavens write your glorious name:
Where, whenas Death shall all the world subdue,
 Our love shall live, and later life renew.

EDMUND SPENSER, English, 1552/1553–1599

SONNET XVIII

Shall I compare thee to a summer's day?
Thou art more lovely and more temperate:
Rough winds do shake the darling buds of May,
And summer's lease hath all too short a date:
Sometime too hot the eye of heaven shines,
And often is his gold complexion dimm'd;
And every fair from fair sometime declines,
By chance, or nature's changing course untrimm'd;
But thy eternal summer shall not fade,
Nor lose possession of that fair thou ow'st,
Nor shall death brag thou wander'st in his shade,
When in eternal lines to time thou grow'st,
  So long as men can breathe, or eyes can see,
  So long lives this, and this gives life to thee.

   WILLIAM SHAKESPEARE, English, 1564–1616

Fleur de Lis. Robert Lewis Reid, American, 1862–1929.
Oil on canvas, ca. 1895–1900.

The Beach at Sainte-Adresse. Claude Monet, French,
1840–1926. Oil on canvas, 1867.

WHERE DOES THIS TENDERNESS COME FROM?

Where does this tenderness come from?
These are not the—first curls I
have stroked slowly—and lips I
have known are—darker than yours

as stars rise often and go out again
(where does this tenderness come from?)
so many eyes have risen and died out
      in front of these eyes of mine.

and yet no such song have
I heard in the darkness of night before,
(where does this tenderness come from?):
      here, on the ribs of the singer.

Where does this tenderness come from?
And what shall I do with it, young
sly singer, just passing by?
Your lashes are—longer than anyone's.

MARINA TSVETAYEVA, Russian, 1892–1941

SONG: TO CELIA

Drink to me, only, with thine eyes,
      And I will pledge with mine;
Or leave a kiss but in the cup,
      And I'll not look for wine.
The thirst, that from the soul doth rise,
      Doth ask a drink divine:
But might I of Jove's nectar sup,
      I would not change for thine.
I sent thee, late, a rosy wreath,
      Not so much honouring thee,
As giving it a hope, that there
      It could not withered be.
But thou thereon did'st only breath,
      And sent'st it back to me:
Since when it grows, and smells, I swear,
      Not of itself, but thee.

BEN JONSON, English, ca. 1572–1637

Venus and Adonis. Detail of
a tapestry designed by Pierre
de Sève the Younger (French,
ca. 1623–1695), Gobelins,
France. Wool, silk, and silver
thread, 1686–92.

Elizabeth Farren (born about 1759, died 1829), Later Countess of Derby. Sir Thomas Lawrence, British, 1769–1830. Oil on canvas, 1790.

SHE WALKS IN BEAUTY

She walks in beauty, like the night
    Of cloudless climes and starry skies;
And all that's best of dark and bright
    Meet in her aspect and her eyes:
Thus mellow'd to that tender light
    Which heaven to gaudy day denies.

One shade the more, one ray the less,
    Had half impaired the nameless grace
Which waves in every raven tress,
    Or softly lightens o'er her face;
Where thoughts serenely sweet express
    How pure, how dear their dwelling-place.

And on that cheek, and o'er that brow,
    So soft, so calm, yet eloquent,
The smiles that win, the tints that glow,
    But tell of days in goodness spent,
A mind at peace with all below,
    A heart whose love is innocent!

        LORD BYRON, English, 1788–1824

LOVE POEM

My child—Star—you gaze at the stars,
and I wish I were the firmament
that I might watch you with many eyes.

        PLATO, Greek, 427–347 B.C.

A DRINKING SONG

Wine comes in at the mouth
And love comes in at the eye:
That's all we shall know for truth
Before we grow old and die.
I lift the glass to my mouth,
I look at you, and I sigh.

WILLIAM BUTLER YEATS, Irish, 1865–1939

A RED, RED ROSE

O my Luve's like a red, red rose,
    That's newly sprung in June;
O my Luve's like the melodie
    That's sweetly play'd in tune.—

As fair art thou, my bonie lass,
    So deep in luve am I;
And I will love thee still, my Dear,
    Till a' the seas gang dry.—

Till a' the seas gang dry, my Dear,
    And the rocks melt wi' the sun:
I will love thee still, my Dear,
    While the sands o' life shall run.—

And fare thee weel, my only Luve!
    And fare thee weel, a while!
And I will come again, my Luve,
    Tho' it were ten thousand mile!

ROBERT BURNS, Scottish, 1759–1796

A Waitress at Duval's Restaurant. Pierre Auguste
Renoir, French, 1841–1919. Oil on canvas, ca. 1875.

Merry Company on a Terrace (detail). Jan Steen, Dutch, 1626–1679. Oil on canvas, ca. 1668–70.

STELLA'S BIRTH-DAY

Stella this day is thirty-four,
(We shan't dispute a year or more:)
However, Stella, be not troubled,
Although thy size and years are doubled
Since first I saw thee at sixteen,
The brightest virgin on the green;
So little is thy form declined;
Made up so largely in thy mind.
O, would it please the gods to split
Thy beauty, size, and years, and wit!
No age could furnish out a pair
Of nymphs so graceful, wise, and fair;
With half the lustre of your eyes,
With half your wit, your years, and size.
And then, before it grew too late,
How should I beg of gentle fate,
(That either nymph might have her swain,)
To split my worship too in twain.

JONATHAN SWIFT, English, 1667–1745

YOUR BIRTHDAY COMES TO TELL ME THIS

your birthday comes to tell me this

—each luckiest of lucky days
i've loved, shall love, do love you, was

and will be and my birthday is

E. E. CUMMINGS, American, 1894–1962

Le Coeur. Henri Matisse, French, 1869–1954. Pochoir from *Jazz*, published by Tériade, Paris, 1947.

A VERY VALENTINE

Very fine is my valentine.
Very fine and very mine.
Very mine is my valentine very mine and very fine.
Very fine is my valentine and mine, very fine very
   mine and mine is my valentine.

GERTRUDE STEIN, American, 1874–1946

SOMEWHERE I HAVE NEVER TRAVELLED

somewhere i have never travelled, gladly beyond
any experience, your eyes have their silence:
in your most frail gesture are things which
      enclose me,
or which i cannot touch because they are too near

your slightest look easily will unclose me
though i have closed myself as fingers,
you open always petal by petal myself as Spring
      opens
(touching skilfully, mysteriously) her first rose

or if your wish be to close me, i and
my life will shut very beautifully, suddenly,
as when the heart of this flower imagines
the snow carefully everywhere descending;

nothing which we are to perceive in this world
      equals
the power of your intense fragility: whose texture
compels me with the colour of its countries,
rendering death and forever with each breathing

(i do not know what it is about you that closes
and opens; only something in me understands
the voice of your eyes is deeper than all roses)
nobody, not even the rain, has such small hands

E. E. CUMMINGS, American, 1894–1962

[78]

The Garden at Vaucresson.
Edouard Vuillard, French,
1868–1940. Distemper on canvas,
1923 and 1937.

PORTRAIT OF A LADY

Your thighs are appletrees
whose blossoms touch the sky.
Which sky? The sky
where Watteau hung a lady's
slipper. Your knees
are a southern breeze—or
a gust of snow. Agh! what
sort of man was Fragonard?
—as if that answered
anything. Ah, yes—below
the knees, since the tune

drops that way, it is
one of those white summer days,
the tall grass of your ankles
flickers upon the shore—
Which shore?—
the sand clings to my lips—
Which shore?
Agh, petals maybe. How
should I know?
Which shore? Which shore?
I said petals from an appletree.

WILLIAM CARLOS WILLIAMS, American, 1883–1963

VARIATION

That still pool of the air
under the branch of an echo.

That still pool of the water
under a frond of bright stars.

That still pool of your mouth
under a thicket of kisses.

FEDERICO GARCÍA LORCA, Spanish, 1899–1936

I WANT TO BREATHE

you in I'm not talking about
perfume or even the sweet o-

dour of your skin but of the
air itself I want to share

your air inhaling what you
exhale I'd like to be that

close two of us breathing
each other as one as that.

JAMES LAUGHLIN, American, b. 1914

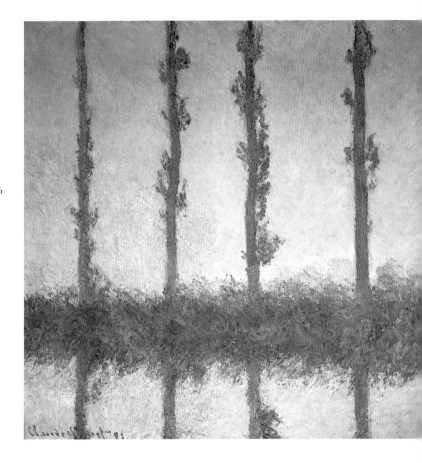

Summer. Frederick Carl Frieseke, American, 1874–1939.
Oil on canvas, 1914.

Poplars. Claude Monet, French, 1840–1926. Oil on canvas,
1891.

FOR AN AMOROUS LADY

"Most mammals like caresses, in the sense
in which we usually take the word,
whereas other creatures, even tame snakes,
prefer giving to receiving them."
FROM A NATURAL-HISTORY BOOK

The pensive gnu, the staid aardvark,
Accept caresses in the dark;
The bear, equipped with paw and snout,
Would rather take than dish it out.
But snakes, both poisonous and garter,
In love are never known to barter;
The worm, though dank, is sensitive:
His noble nature bids him *give*.

But you, my dearest, have a soul
Encompassing fish, flesh, and fowl.
When amorous arts we would pursue,
You can, with pleasure, bill *or* coo.
You are, in truth, one in a million,
At once mammalian and reptilian.

THEODORE ROETHKE, American, 1908–1963

LADY LOVE

She is standing on my lids
And her hair is in my hair
She has the colour of my eye
She has the body of my hand
In my shade she is engulfed
As a stone against the sky

She will never close her eyes
And she does not let me sleep
And her dreams in the bright day
Make the suns evaporate
And me laugh cry and laugh
Speak when I have nothing to say

PAUL ELUARD, French, 1895–1952

Stepping Out. Roy Lichtenstein, American, b. 1923.
Oil and Magna on canvas, 1978. © Roy Lichtenstein.

TO YOU

I love you as a sheriff searches for a walnut
That will solve a murder case unsolved for years
Because the murderer left it in the snow beside a window
Through which he saw her head, connecting with
Her shoulders by a neck, and laid a red
Roof in her heart. For this we live a thousand years;
For this we love, and we live because we love, we are not
Inside a bottle, thank goodness! I love you as a
Kid searches for a goat; I am crazier than shirttails
In the wind, when you're near, a wind that blows from
The big blue sea, so shiny so deep and so unlike us;
I think I am bicycling across an Africa of green and
    white fields
Always, to be near you, even in my heart
When I'm awake, which swims, and also I believe
    that you
Are trustworthy as the sidewalk which leads me to
The place where I again think of you, a new
Harmony of thoughts! I love you as the sunlight
    leads the prow
Of a ship which sails
From Hartford to Miami, and I love you
Best at dawn, when even before I am awake the sun
Receives me in the questions which you always pose.

    KENNETH KOCH, American, b. 1924

Lovers Under Lilies. Marc Chagall, French (b. in Russia), 1887–1985. Oil on canvas, 1922–25.

[83]

Woman with a Pink. Rembrandt Harmensz van Rijn,
Dutch, 1606–1669. Oil on canvas.

THE CONFIRMATION

Yes, yours, my love, is the right human face.
I in my mind had waited for this long,
Seeing the false and searching for the true,
Then found you as a traveller finds a place
Of welcome suddenly amid the wrong
Valleys and rocks and twisting roads. But you,
What shall I call you? A fountain in a waste,
A well of water in a country dry,
Or anything that's honest and good, an eye
That makes the whole world bright. Your open
    heart,
Simple with giving, gives the primal deed,
The first good world, the blossom, the blowing
    seed,
The hearth, the steadfast land, the wandering
    sea,
Not beautiful or rare in every part,
But like yourself, as they were meant to be.

EDWIN MUIR, Scottish, 1887–1959

The Mess of Love

Dubo, Dubon, Dubonnet. André Kertész, American
(b. in Hungary), 1894–1985. Gelatin silver print, 1934.

THE MESS OF LOVE

We've made a great mess of love
Since we made an ideal of it.

The moment I swear to love a woman, a certain
    woman, all my life
That moment I begin to hate her.

The moment I even say to a woman: I love you!—
My love dies down considerably.

The moment love is an understood thing between
    us, we are sure of it,
It's a cold egg, it isn't love any more.

Love is like a flower, it must flower and fade;
If it doesn't fade, it is not a flower,
It's either an artificial rag blossom, or an
    immortelle, for the cemetery.

The moment the mind interferes with love, or the
    will fixes on it,
Or the personality assumes it as an attribute, or
    the ego takes possession of it,
It is not love any more, it's just a mess.
And we've made a great mess of love, mind-
    perverted, will-perverted, ego-perverted love.

        D. H. Lawrence, English, 1885–1930

I AM NO GOOD AT LOVE

I am no good at love
My heart should be wise and free
I kill the unfortunate golden goose
Whoever it may be
With over-articulate tenderness
And too much intensity.

I am no good at love
I batter it out of shape
Suspicion tears at my sleepless mind
And, gibbering like an ape,
I lie alone in the endless dark
Knowing there's no escape.

I am no good at love
When my easy heart I yield
Wild words come tumbling from my mouth
Which should have stayed concealed;
And my jealousy turns a bed of bliss
Into a battlefield.

I am no good at love
I betray it with little sins
For I feel the misery of the end
In the moment that it begins
And the bitterness of the last good-bye
Is the bitterness that wins.

       NOEL COWARD, English, 1899–1973

Mezzetin. Jean Antoine Watteau, French, 1684–1721.
Oil on canvas.

Prudence. Andrea della Robbia, Italian (Florentine), 1435–1525. Glazed terracotta relief, ca. 1475.

Wall. Detail of a bedroom wall from the villa of P. Fannius Synistor at Boscoreale. Roman, 40–30 B.C. Fresco on lime plaster.

I CAN'T HOLD YOU AND I CAN'T LEAVE YOU

I can't hold you and I can't leave you,
and sorting the reasons to leave you or hold you,
I find an intangible one to love you,
and many tangible ones to forgo you.

As you won't change, nor let me forgo you,
I shall give my heart a defence against you,
so that half shall always be armed to abhor you,
though the other half be ready to adore you.

Then, if our love, by loving flourish,
let it not in endless feuding perish;
let us speak no more in jealousy and suspicion.

He offers not part, who would all receive—
so know that when it is your intention
mine shall be to make believe.

JUANA INÉS DELA CRUZ, Mexican, 1651–1695

[88]

THE STREET IN SHADOW

The street in shadow. Tall houses hide
the dying sun; in balconies are echoes of light.

Do you see in the spell of the flowery window
the pink oval of a familiar face?

The image behind the distorting glass
looms or fades like an old daguerreotype.

In the street, only the patter of your step;
echoes of the sunset slowly burn out.

Agony! Pain hangs in my heart. Is it she?
It cannot be. Walk on. In the blue, a star.

Antonio Machado Ruiz, Spanish, 1875–1939

ROOMS

I remember rooms that have had their part
    In the steady slowing down of the heart.
The room in Paris, the room at Geneva,
The little damp room with the seaweed smell,
And that ceaseless maddening sound of the tide—
    Rooms where for good or for ill—things died.
But there is the room where we (two) lie dead,
Though every morning we seem to wake and
    might just as well seem to sleep again
        As we shall somewhere in the other quieter,
         dustier bed
        Out there in the sun—in the rain.

Charlotte Mew, English, 1870–1928

SHE'S GAZING AT YOU SO TENDERLY

She's gazing at you so tenderly,
Drowning you in sparkling conversation,
Gay and witty, and her eyes
Absorbing you with their yearning.
But last night she was using all her skill
To give me secretly her little foot
Under the tablecloth for me to caress.

ALEXANDER PUSHKIN, Russian, 1799–1837

MY WOMAN

My woman says she wants no other lover
    than me, not even Jupiter himself.
She says so. What a woman says to an eager
  sweetheart
    write on the wind, write on the rushing
    waves.

CATULLUS, Roman, ca. 84–54 B.C.

Lovers, Place d'Italie. Brassaï (Gyula Halász), French (b. in Transylvania), 1899–1984. Gelatin silver print, ca. 1932; print ca. 1970.

The Fortune Teller. Georges de La Tour, French, 1593–1652. Oil on canvas.

WHEN LOVE FLIES IN

When Love flies in,   Nor make no sign
Make—make no sign;   If love flit out;
Owl-soft his wings,   He'll tire of thee
Sand-blind his eyes;   Without a doubt.
Sigh, if thou must,   Stifle thy pangs;
But seal him thine.   Thy heart resign;
                    And live without!

WALTER DE LA MARE, English, 1873–1956

WHEN I WAS ONE-AND-TWENTY

When I was one-and-twenty
    I heard a wise man say,
"Give crowns and pounds and guineas
    But not your heart away;
Give pearls away and rubies
    But keep your fancy free."
But I was one-and-twenty,
    No use to talk to me.

When I was one-and-twenty
    I heard him say again,
"The heart out of the bosom
    Was never given in vain;
'Tis paid with sighs a plenty
    And sold for endless rue."
And I am two-and-twenty,
    And oh, 'tis true, 'tis true.

A. E. HOUSMAN, English, 1859–1936

The Englishman at the Moulin Rouge. Henri de
Toulouse-Lautrec, French, 1864–1901. Color lithograph,
1892.

Kiesler and Wife. Will Barnet, American, b. 1911. Oil on
canvas, 1963–65.

SONG

Go and catch a falling star,
　　Get with child a mandrake root,
Tell me where all past years are,
　　Or who cleft the Devil's foot,
Teach me to hear mermaids singing,
Or to keep off envy's stinging,
　　　　And find
　　　　What wind
Serves to advance an honest mind.

If thou beest born to strange sights,
　　Things invisible to see,
Ride ten thousand days and nights,
　　Till age snow white hairs on thee.
Thou, when thou return'st, wilt tell me
All strange wonders that befell thee,
　　　　And swear
　　　　Nowhere
Lives a woman true, and fair.

If thou find'st one, let me know,
　　Such a pilgrimage were sweet;
Yet do not, I would not go,
　　Though at next door we might meet;
Though she were true when you met her,
And last till you write your letter,
　　　　Yet she
　　　　Will be
False, ere I come, to two, or three.

JOHN DONNE, English, 1572–1631

[92]

WEARING THE COLLAR

I live with a lady and four cats
and some days we all get
along.

some days I have trouble with
one of the
cats.

other days I have trouble with
two of the
cats.

other days,
three.

some days I have trouble with
all four of the
cats

and the
lady:

ten eyes looking at me
as if I was a dog.

Charles Bukowski, American, b. 1920

PARTING

Our love has been dying for years.
And now our parting
suddenly resurrects it.
Our love rises from the dead
uncanny
as a corpse which came to life in order to die
for the second time.

Every night we make love,
every hour we are parting,
every hour
we swear to each other faith till the grave.

We suffer intensively,
as one suffers in hell.
Each of us runs
a 110 fever.

Moaning out of hatred
we pluck our wedding photograph from the album
And every night till dawn,
crying, making love,
breaking into cold sweat,
we talk to each other,
we talk to each other,
we talk to each other,
for the first and the last time in life.

ANNA SWIR, Polish, 1909–1984

The Dressing Room.
Pierre Bonnard, French,
1867–1947. Oil on
canvas, 1914.

Woman with Chrysanthemums
(Madame Paul Valpinçon?).
Edgar Degas, French,
1834–1917. Oil on canvas, 1865.

CHANCE

Chance says,
come here,
chance says,
can you bear

to part?
chance says,
sweetheart,
we haven't loved

for almost a year,
can you bear
this loneliness?
I can't;

apart from you,
I fear
wind,
bird,

sea,
wave,
low places
and the high air;

I hear
dire threat
everywhere;
I start

at wind
in sycamores,
I can't bear
anything

further;
chance says,
dear,
I'm here,

don't you want me
any more?

H.D. (HILDA DOOLITTLE),
American, 1886–1961

Office in a Small City. Edward Hopper, American, 1882–1967. Oil on canvas, 1953.

Stargazers. Engraving from *Ethica naturalis, seu documenta moralia*, written by Christopher Weigel (German). Published in Nuremberg, ca. 1700.

LONELINESS

To think of you surcharged with
Loneliness. To hear your voice
Over the recorder say,
"Loneliness." The word, the voice,
So full of it, and I, with
You away, so lost in it—
Lost in loneliness and pain.
Black and unendurable,
Thinking of you with every
Corpuscle of my flesh, in
Every instant of night
And day. O, my love, the times
We have forgotten love, and
Sat lonely beside each other.
We have eaten together,
Lonely behind our plates, we
Have hidden behind children,
We have slept together in
A lonely bed. Now my heart
Turns towards you, awake at last,
Penitent, lost in the last
Loneliness. Speak to me. Talk
To me. Break the black silence.
Speak of a tree full of leaves,
Of a flying bird, the new
Moon in the sunset, a poem,
A book, a person—all the
Casual healing speech
Of your resonant, quiet voice.
The word freedom. The word peace.

KENNETH REXROTH, American, 1905–1982

THE MORE LOVING ONE

Looking up at the stars, I know quite well
That, for all they care, I can go to hell,
But on earth indifference is the least
We have to dread from man or beast.

How should we like it were stars to burn
With a passion for us we could not return?
If equal affection cannot be,
Let the more loving one be me.

Admirer as I think I am
Of stars that do not give a damn,
I cannot, now I see them, say
I missed one terribly all day.

Were all stars to disappear or die,
I should learn to look at an empty sky
And feel its total dark sublime,
Though this might take me a little time.

W. H. AUDEN, American (b. England), 1907–1973

3 LITTLE POEMS

I call you on
the 'phone &
we chat, but
the way tele
is missing from
'phone is the
way it makes me
feel, wishing
the rest of
you were here.

In literature and song
love is often expressed
in the imagery of
weather. For example,
"Now that we are one
Clouds won't hide our sun.
There'll be blue skies . . .
etc." Partly cloudy
and cool today, high
around fifty, mostly
cloudy tonight and tomorrow.

4:50 and dark
already? Everyone
wants to be
beautiful but
few are. 4:51
and darker.

RON PADGETT, American, b. 1942

Telephone Booths.
Richard Estes, American, b. 1936.
Acrylic on Masonite, 1967.

CRYSTAL PALACE MARKET

House of Fire. James Rosenquist,
American, b. 1933. Oil
on canvas, 1981.

Saw a girl in a food
store that looked like

giant food market full
of things to eat every

you gave me the shakes
in my poor old heart

thing to eat that a
person could desire

darling darling sings
the voice on the radio

but I guess that I'll go
hungry hungry hungry

darling why did we
ever drift apart big

darling says the radio
why did we ever part?

JAMES LAUGHLIN, American, b. 1914

[99]

"IF ONLY I KNEW THE TRUTH, I SWEAR I WOULD ACT ON IT—"

On the tedious ferry crossing through
   the obscure night
toward the darkly lurid dock at Barclay Street
on the dark Hudson River pelted by the rain
the orange lightnings thick silently flickered
   and flashed
there was no thunderclap
I was sick with ignorance and fear

not knowing if my wife had left me, not knowing
   if I wanted that
was I making a waste for spite, and wise too late, if at all?
"If only I knew the truth, I swear I would act on it!"
I was in confusion and fright
the rain was pounding the water
the lightning was obscure
there came no thunderclap
the boat did not seem to advance.

PAUL GOODMAN, American, 1911–1972

A Storm. Georgia O'Keeffe,
American, 1887–1986.
Pastel on paper, 1922.

**Study for Sunday
Afternoon on the Island
of La Grande Jatte** (detail).
Georges Seurat, French,
1859–1891. Oil on wood.

LOVE IS A SECRET FEEDING FIRE

Love is a secret feeding fire that gives all
    creatures being,
Life to the dead, speech to the dumb, and to the
    blind man seeing.
And yet in me he contradicts all these his sacred
    graces:
Sears up my lips, my eyes, my life, and from me
    ever flying
Leads me in paths untracked, ungone, and many
    uncouth places,
Where in despair I beauty curse. Curse love and
    all fair faces!

        Anonymous, English

SOFTLY

Softly Baby I'll stop having a thing for you.
Softly I'll try not to call again.
And even if I do, I'll realize
It's not such a good idea.

Softly I'll learn that what I thought was true.
For a soft while I'll be asleep by ten.
I won't look at everything just through your eyes,
And I'll softly try not to see ya.

        John White, American, b. 1958

The Bridge at Villeneuve-la-Garenne. Alfred Sisley, British, 1839–1899. Oil on canvas, 1872.

MIRABEAU BRIDGE

Under the Mirabeau Bridge there flows the Seine
    Must I recall
  Our loves recall how then
After each sorrow joy came back again

    Let night come on bells end the day
    The days go by me still I stay

Hands joined and face to face let's stay just so
    While underneath
  The bridge of our arms shall go
Weary of endless looks the river's flow

    Let night come on bells end the day
    The days go by me still I stay

All love goes by as water to the sea
    All love goes by
  How slow life seems to me
How violent the hope of love can be

    Let night come on bells end the day
    The days go by me still I stay

The days the weeks pass by beyond our ken
    Neither time past
  Nor love comes back again
Under the Mirabeau Bridge there flows the Seine

    Let night come on bells end the day
    The days go by me still I stay

GUILLAUME APOLLINAIRE, French, 1880–1918

Yesterday He Still Looked in My Eyes

YESTERDAY HE STILL
LOOKED IN MY EYES

Yesterday he still looked in my eyes, yet
    today   his looks are bent aside.   Yesterday
he sat here until the birds began, but
    today   all those larks are   ravens.

Stupid creature! And you are wise, you
    live while I am stunned.
Now for the lament of women in all times:
    —My love, what was it I did to you?

And tears are   water, blood is   water,
    a woman always washes in blood and tears.
Love is a step-mother, and no mother:
    then expect no justice or mercy from her.

Ships carry away the ones we love.
    Along the white road they are taken away.
And one cry stretches across the earth:
    —My love, what was it I did to you?

Yesterday he lay at my feet. He even
    compared me with the Chinese empire! Then
suddenly he let his hands fall open, and
    my life fell out like   a rusty kopeck.

A child-murderer, before some court
    I stand   loathsome and timid I am.
And yet even in Hell I shall demand:
    —My love, what was it I did to you?

I ask this chair, I ask the bed: Why?
    Why do I suffer and live in penury?
His kisses stopped. He wanted to break you.
    To kiss another girl is their reply.

He taught me to live in fire, he threw me there,
    and then abandoned me on steppes of ice.
My love, I know what you have done to me.
    —My love, what was it I did to you?

I know everything, don't argue with me!
    I can see now, I'm a lover no longer.
And now I know wherever love holds power
    Death approaches soon   like a gardener.

It is almost like shaking a tree, in time
    some ripe apple comes falling down. So
for everything, for everything   forgive me,
    —my love   whatever it was I did to you.

MARINA TSVETAYEVA, Russian, 1892–1941

The Letter. Jean Baptiste Camille Corot, French, 1796–1875. Oil on wood.

FAREWELL
UNGRATEFUL TRAITOR

Farewell ungrateful traitor,
    Farewell my perjured swain,
Let never injured creature
    Believe a man again.
The pleasure of possessing
Surpasses all expressing,
But 'tis too short a blessing,
    And love too long a pain.

'Tis easy to deceive us
    In pity of your pain,
But when we love you leave us
    To rail at you in vain.
Before we have descried it,
There is no bliss beside it,
But she that once has tried it
    Will never love again.

The passion you pretended
    Was only to obtain,
But when the charm is ended
    The charmer you disdain.
Your love by ours we measure
Till we have lost our treasure,
But dying is a pleasure,
    When living is a pain.

JOHN DRYDEN, English, 1631–1700

THE STARS STAND UP IN THE AIR

The stars stand up in the air
The sun and the moon are gone,
The strand of its waters is bare,
And her sway is swept from the swan.

The cuckoo was calling all day,
Hid in the branches above,
How my storin is fled away,
'Tis my grief that I gave her my love!

Three things through love I see—
Sorrow and sin and death—
And my mind reminding me
That this doom I breathe with my breath.

But sweeter than violin or lute
Is my love—and she left me behind.
I wish that all music were mute,
And I to my beauty were blind.

She's more shapely than swan by the strand,
She's more radiant than grass after dew,
She's more fair than the stars where they stand—
'Tis my grief that her ever I knew!

ANONYMOUS, Irish

The Coming Storm. Martin Johnson Heade, American,
1819–1904. Oil on canvas, 1859.

[106]

SOUVENIRS

my love has left me has gone from me
    and I with no keepsake nothing
    not a glove handkerchief lock of hair picture
    only in memory

the first night the magic snowfall
    the warm blue-walled room we looking out at
      the snow
    listening to music drinking the same cocktail
    she pressing my hand searching my eyes
    the first kiss my hands touching her
    she close to me answering my lips
    waking at morning eyes opening slowly

I approaching her house trembling
    kissing her entering the room
    waking all night writing a poem for her
    thinking of her planning her pleasure
    remembering her least liking and desire
    she cooking for me eating with me
    kissing me with little kisses over the face
    we telling our lives till morning

more to remember better to forget
    she denying me slashing my love
    all pain forgotten if only she comes back to me

    DUDLEY RANDALL, American, b. 1914

Old Souvenirs. John Frederick Peto, American, 1854–1907.
Oil on canvas, ca. 1881–1901.

ALONE IN HER BEAUTY

Who is lovelier than she?
Yet she lives alone in an empty valley.
She tells me she came from a good family
Which is humbled now into the dust.
. . . When trouble arose in the Kuan district,
Her brothers and close kin were killed.
What use were their high offices,
Not even shielding their own lives?—
The world has but scorn for adversity;
Hope goes out, like the light of a candle.
Her husband, with a vagrant heart,
Seeks a new face like a new piece of jade;
And when morning-glories furl at night
And mandarin-ducks lie side by side,
All he can see is the smile of the new love,
While the old love weeps unheard.
The brook was pure in its mountain source,
But away from the mountain its waters darken.
. . . Waiting for her maid to come from
    selling pearls
For straw to cover the roof again,
She picks a few flowers, no longer for her hair,
And lets pine-needles fall through her fingers,
And, forgetting her thin silk sleeve and the cold,
She leans in the sunset by a tall bamboo.

Tu Fu, Chinese, 712–770

Girl with Lantern on a Balcony at Night. Suzuki
Harunobu, Japanese, 1725–1770. Woodblock print in colors,
ca. 1768.

A LOON I THOUGHT IT WAS

A loon I thought it was,
But it was my love's splashing oar.
To Sault Ste. Marie he has departed,
My love has gone on before me,
Never again can I see him.
A loon I thought it was,
But it was my love's splashing oar.

       ANONYMOUS, Chippewa Indian

Courtesan Holding a Fan. Kitagawa Utamaro,
Japanese, 1753(?)–1806. Woodblock print in colors.

THE REJECTED WIFE

Entering the Hall, she meets the new wife;
Leaving the gate, she runs into former husband.
Words stick; does not manage to say anything.
Presses hands together; stands hesitating.
Agitates moon-like fan, sheds pearl-like tears,
Realizes she loves him as much as ever,
Present pain never come to an end.

      ANONYMOUS, China

Peach Blossoms—Villiers le Bel. Childe Hassam,
American, 1859–1935. Oil on canvas.

THE SPRING AND THE FALL

In the spring of the year, in the spring of the year,
I walked the road beside my dear.
The trees were black where the bark was wet.
I see them yet, in the spring of the year.
He broke me a bough of the blossoming peach
That was out of the way and hard to reach.

In the fall of the year, in the fall of the year,
I walked the road beside my dear.
The rooks went up with a raucous trill.
I hear them still, in the fall of the year.
He laughed at all I dared to praise,
And broke my heart, in little ways.

Year be springing or year be falling,
The bark will drip and the birds be calling.
There's much that's fine to see and hear
In the spring of a year, in the fall of a year.
'Tis not love's going hurts my days,
But that it went in little ways.

EDNA ST. VINCENT MILLAY, American, 1892–1950

**Mademoiselle Marie Dihau
(1843–1935)**. Edgar Degas, French,
1834–1917. Oil on canvas.

I DO NOT LOOK FOR LOVE THAT IS A DREAM

I do not look for love that is a dream—
    I only seek for courage to be still;
    To bear my grief with an unbending will,
And when I am a-weary not to seem.
Let the round world roll on; let the sun beam;
    Let the wind blow, and let the rivers fill
    The everlasting sea, and on the hill
The palms almost touch heaven, as children
    deem.

And, though young spring and summer pass away,
    And autumn and cold winter come again,
    And though my soul, being tired of its pain,
Pass from the ancient earth, and though my clay
    Return to dust, my tongue shall not
    complain;—
No man shall mock me after this my day.

        Christina Rossetti, English, 1830–1894

The Letter. Mary Cassatt, American, 1844–1926. Drypoint and aquatint printed in color, 1890–91.

RESPONSE

When you wrote your letter it was April,
And you were glad that it was spring weather,
And that the sun shone out in turn with showers
    of rain.

I write in waning May and it is autumn,
And I am glad that my chrysanthemums
Are tied up fast to strong posts,
So that the south winds cannot beat them down.
I am glad that they are tawny coloured,
And fiery in the low west evening light.
And I am glad that one bush warbler
Still sings in the honey-scented wattle . . .

But oh, we have remembering hearts,
And we say "How green it was in such and such
    an April,"
And "Such and such an autumn was very golden,"
And "Everything is for a very short time."

        MARY URSULA BETHELL, New Zealand, 1874–1945

In the Woods. Asher Brown Durand, American, 1796–1886. Oil on canvas, 1855.

THE IMPULSE

It was too lonely for her there,
 And too wild,
And since there were but two of them,
 And no child,

And work was little in the house,
 She was free,
And followed where he furrowed field,
 Or felled tree.

She rested on a log and tossed
 The fresh chips,
With a song only to herself
 On her lips.

And once she went to break a bough
 Of black alder.
She strayed so far she scarcely heard
 When he called her—

And didn't answer—didn't speak—
 Or return.
She stood, and then she ran and hid
 In the fern.

He never found her, though he looked
 Everywhere,
And he asked at her mother's house
 Was she there.

Sudden and swift and light as that
 The ties gave,
And he learned of finalities
 Besides the grave.

ROBERT FROST, American, 1874–1963

I WALKED PAST A HOUSE
WHERE I LIVED ONCE

I walked past a house where I lived once:
a man and a woman are still together in the
    whispers there.
Many years have passed with the quiet hum
of the staircase bulb going on
and off and on again.

The keyholes are like little wounds
where all the blood seeped out. And inside,
people pale as death.

I want to stand once again as I did
holding my first love all night long in the doorway.
When we left at dawn, the house
began to fall apart and since then the city and
    since then
the whole world.

I want to be filled with longing again
till dark burn marks show on my skin.

I want to be written again
in the Book of Life, to be written every single day
till the writing hand hurts.

       YEHUDA AMICHAI, Israeli, b. 1924

A RANT

"What you wanted I told you"
I said "and what you left me
I took! Don't stand around
my bedroom making things cry

any more! I'm not going to
thrash the floor or throw any
apples! To hell with the radio,
let it rot! I'm not going to be

the monster in my own bed
any more!" Well. The silence
was too easily arrived at; most
oppressive. The pictures swung

on the wall with boredom and
the plants imagined us all in
Trinidad. I was crowded with
windows. I raced to the door.

"Come back" I cried "for a minute!
You left your new shoes. And the
coffee pot's yours!" There were no
footsteps. Wow! what a relief!

       FRANK O'HARA, American, 1926–1966

Thursday. John Moore, American, b. 1941. Oil on canvas, 1980.

A SPRING NIGHT IN SHOKOKU-JI

Eight years ago this May
We walked under cherry blossoms
At night in an orchard in Oregon.
All that I wanted then
Is forgotten now, but you.
Here in the night
In a garden of the old capital
I feel the trembling ghost of Yugao
I remember your cool body
Naked under a summer cotton dress.

GARY SNYDER, American, b. 1930

THE NIGHT HAS A THOUSAND EYES

The night has a thousand eyes,
    And the day but one;
Yet the light of the bright world dies
    With the dying sun.

The mind has a thousand eyes,
    And the heart but one;
Yet the light of a whole life dies
    When love is done.

FRANCIS WILLIAM BOURDILLON, English,
1852–1921

Oriental Pleasure Garden. Paul Klee, German, 1879–1940. Oil on cardboard, 1925.

L'Arlésienne: Madame Joseph-Michel Ginoux (Marie Julien, 1848–1911). Vincent van Gogh, Dutch, 1853–1890.

WESTERN WIND, WHEN WILL THOU BLOW

Western wind, when will thou blow
    The small rain down can rain?
Christ, if my love were in my arms
    And I in my bed again!

Anonymous, English, 16th century

WHEN YOU ARE OLD

When you are old and grey and full of sleep,
And nodding by the fire, take down this book,
And slowly read, and dream of the soft look
Your eyes had once, and of their shadows deep;

How many loved your moments of glad grace,
And loved your beauty with love false or true,
But one man loved the pilgrim soul in you,
And loved the sorrows of your changing face;

And bending down beside the glowing bars,
Murmur, a little sadly, how Love fled
And paced upon the mountains overhead
And hid his face amid a crowd of stars.

William Butler Yeats, Irish, 1865–1939

JOYS THAT STING

Oh doe not die, says Donne, *for I shall hate*
All women so. How false the sentence rings.
Women? But in a life made desolate
It is the joys once shared that have the stings.

To take the old walks alone, or not at all,
To order one pint where I ordered two,
To think of, and then not to make, the small
Time-honoured joke (senseless to all but you);

To laugh (oh, one'll laugh), to talk upon
Themes that we talked upon when you were
    there,
To make some poor pretence of going on,
Be kind to one's old friends, and seem to care,

While no one (O God) through the years will say
The simplest, common word in just your way.

C. S. Lewis, English, 1898–1963

The Green Blouse. Pierre Bonnard, French, 1867–1947.
Oil on canvas, 1919.

Spring Showers, New York, 1900. Alfred Stieglitz,
American, 1864–1946. Photogravure.

RAIN

A sad sort of rain,
Today, and I inside, alone,
Look at the pictures I took of you
In London and Paris and Spain.

What good will it do
This dark gray mood
To try to think back
To that sunlit blue?
Better to clean,
Bake bread,
And feed the fire,
So when our sons come home
From school,
The house will feel warm,
Unclouded, serene.

No one must see the ghost
Of me that wanders
Over the field and wood
Above this thin rain,
Filled with an ache
And a crazy refrain.

Never again
Never again
We two at the farm
Or in London or Spain.
But under some other moon
Maybe?
Under some unknown sun,
Again, we two, we two might be
Always again?

MARGARET NEWLIN, American, b. 1925

SOMETIMES WITH ONE I LOVE

Sometimes with one I love I fill myself with rage
    for fear I effuse unreturn'd love,
But now I think there is no unreturn'd love, the
    pay is certain one way or another,
(I loved a certain person ardently and my love was
    not return'd,
Yet out of that I have written these songs.)

        WALT WHITMAN, American, 1819–1892

Woman Playing the Kithara. From the Villa of P. Fannius
Synistor at Boscoreale. Roman, 40–30 B.C. Fresco on lime
plaster.

PAST ONE O'CLOCK ...

Past one o'clock. You must have gone to bed.
The Milky Way streams silver through the night.
I'm in no hurry; with lightning telegrams
I have no cause to wake or trouble you.
And, as they say, the incident is closed.
Love's boat has smashed against the daily grind.
Now you and I are quits. Why bother then
to balance mutual sorrows, pains, and hurts.
Behold what quiet settles on the world.
Night wraps the sky in tribute from the stars.
In hours like these, one rises to address
The ages, history, and all creation.

        VLADIMIR MAYAKOVSKY, Russian, 1893–1930

TO ——

Music, when soft voices die,
Vibrates in the memory;
Odours, when sweet violets sicken,
Live within the sense they quicken.

Rose leaves, when the rose is dead,
Are heaped for the belovèd's bed;
And so thy thoughts, when thou art gone,
Love itself shall slumber on.

        PERCY BYSSHE SHELLEY, English, 1792–1822

LAMENT

The stars and the rivers
and waves call you back.

PINDAR, Greek,
ca. 522–443 B.C.

Waterfall. Lid of a
writing box. Japanese,
late 18th century.
Sprinkled design on lacquer.

LISTEN, WILL YOU LEARN
TO HEAR ME FROM AFAR

Listen, will you learn to hear me from afar?
It's a question of inclining the heart more than
   the ear.
You'll find bridges in yourself and roads
To reach all the way to me who waits and stares.

What does it matter, the Atlantic's width.
The fields, woods, mountains between us two?
One by one they'll have to give up on that day
You turn your eyes this way.

        JULES SUPERVIELLE, French, 1884–1960

Landscape. Detail from *Virgin and Child*. Joos van Cleve,
Flemish, active by 1507, d. 1540/41. Tempera and oil on
wood, ca. 1525.

The Marriage of True Minds

SONNET CXVI

Let me not to the marriage of true minds
Admit impediments, love is not love
Which alters when it alteration finds,
Or bends with the remover to remove.
O no! it is an ever-fixed mark,
That looks on tempests and is never shaken;
It is the star to every wand'ring bark,
Whose worth's unknown, although his height
   be taken.
Love's not Time's fool, though rosy lips and
   cheeks
Within his bending sickle's compass come,
Love alters not with his brief hours and weeks,
But bears it out even to the edge of doom:
     If this be error and upon me proved,
     I never writ, nor no man ever loved.

WILLIAM SHAKESPEARE, English, 1564–1616

Antoine-Laurent Lavoisier (1743–1794) and His Wife (Marie-Anne Pierrette Paulze, 1758–1836). Jacques Louis David, French, 1748–1825. Oil on canvas.

Memisabu and His Wife. Egyptian, ca. 2360 B.C., Dynasty 5. Painted limestone.

TO MY DEAR AND LOVING HUSBAND

If ever two were one, then surely we.
If ever man were loved by wife, then thee;
If ever wife was happy in a man,
Compare with me, ye women, if you can.
I prize thy love more than whole mines of gold
Or all the riches that the East doth hold.
My love is such that rivers cannot quench,
Nor ought but love from thee, give recompense.
Thy love is such I can no way repay,
The heavens reward thee manifold, I pray.
Then while we live, in love let's so persevere
That when we live no more, we may live ever.

ANNE BRADSTREET, American Colonial,
ca. 1612–1672

ALTHOUGH I CONQUER ALL THE EARTH

Although I conquer all the earth,
Yet for me there is only one city.
In that city there is for me only one house;
And in that house, one room only;
And in that room, a bed.
And one woman sleeps there,
The shining joy and jewel of all my kingdom.

ANONYMOUS, Ancient India

GALANTE GARDEN: I

Spring morning!
She came to kiss me
Just as a morning skylark
Soared up from the furrow singing,
"Spring morning!"

I spoke to her of a white butterfly
That I saw in the footpath;
And she gave me a rose
And said, "How I love you!
Don't you know that I love you?"

So many kisses she cherished
On her red lips for me!
I was kissing her eyelids . . .
"My eyes are for you
And you for my red lips!"

The spring heavens
Were blue with peace and oblivion . . .
A morning skylark
Sang in the still sleeping garden . . .
Its voice was light and crystal
In the newplowed furrow . . .
Spring morning!

JUAN RAMÓN JIMÉNEZ, Spanish, 1881–1958

SONG OF SONGS

I am my lover's and he desires me.
Come, my darling,
let us go out into the fields
and spend the night in villages.
Let us wake early and go to the vineyards
and see if the vine is in blossom,
if the new grape bud is open
and the pomegranates in bloom.

There I will give you my love.
The mandrakes will spray aroma
and over our door will be precious fruit,
new and old,
which I have saved for you, my darling.

THE SONG OF SOLOMON, 7:10–13

QUATRAIN

What is this day with two suns in the sky?
Day unlike other days,
with a great voice giving it to the planet,
Here it is, enamored beings, your day!

JALAL-UD-DIN RUMI, Persian, 1207–1273

Magnolia and Irises
(detail). Tiffany Studios,
New York City, ca. 1905.
Leaded glass.

SO LET'S LIVE—REALLY LIVE!

So let's live–really live!–for love and loving,
honey! Guff of the grumpy old *harrumph!*-ers
–what's it worth? Is it even worth a penny?
Suns go under and bubble bright as ever
up but–smothered, our little light, the night's one
sudden plunge–and oblivion forever.
Kiss me! kiss me a thousand times! A hundred!

Now a thousand again! Another hundred!
Don't stop yet. Add a thousand. And a hundred.
So. Then post, sitting pretty on our millions,
sums that none–we the least–make head or tail of.
Don't let's know, even us. Or evil eyes might
glitter green, over such a spell of kisses.

CATULLUS, Roman, ca. 84–54 B.C.

Bacchanalia. Pablo Picasso, Spanish, 1881–1973. Linoleum
cut, 1959.

ANNIVERSARY ON THE ISLAND

The long waves glide in through the afternoon
while we watch from the island
from the cool shadow under the trees where the
   long ridge
a fold in the skirt of the mountain
runs down to the end of the headland

day after day we wake to the island
the light rises through the drops on the leaves
and we remember like birds where we are
night after night we touch the dark island
that once we set out for

and lie still at last with the island in our arms
hearing the leaves and the breathing shore
there are no years any more
only the one mountain
and on all sides the sea that brought us

       W. S. MERWIN, American, b. 1927

Palm Tree, Nassau. Winslow Homer, American,
1836–1910. Watercolor on paper, 1898.

SHE WAS A PHANTOM OF DELIGHT

She was a Phantom of delight
When first she gleamed upon my sight;
A lovely Apparition, sent
To be a moment's ornament;
Her eyes as stars of Twilight fair;
Like Twilight's, too, her dusky hair;
But all things else about her drawn
From May-time and the cheerful Dawn;
A dancing Shape, an Image gay,
To haunt, to startle, and way-lay.

I saw her upon nearer view,
A Spirit, yet a Woman too!
Her household motions light and free,
And steps of virgin-liberty;
A countenance in which did meet
Sweet records, promises as sweet;
A Creature not too bright or good
For human nature's daily food;
For transient sorrows, simple wiles,
Praise, blame, love, kisses, tears, and smiles.

And now I see with eye serene
The very pulse of the machine;
A Being breathing thoughtful breath,
A Traveller between life and death;
The reason firm, the temperate will,
Endurance, foresight, strength, and skill;
A perfect Woman, nobly planned,
To warn, to comfort, and command;
And yet a Spirit still, and bright
With something of angelic light.

WILLIAM WORDSWORTH, English, 1770–1850

Young Woman with a Water Jug. Johannes Vermeer, Dutch, 1632–1675. Oil on canvas.

A DEDICATION TO MY WIFE

To whom I owe the leaping delight
That quickens my senses in our wakingtime
And the rhythm that governs the repose of our
    sleepingtime,
        The breathing in unison

Of lovers whose bodies smell of each other
Who think the same thoughts without need of
    speech
And babble the same speech without need of
    meaning.

No peevish winter wind shall chill
No sullen tropic sun shall wither
The roses in the rose-garden which is ours and
    ours only

But this dedication is for others to read:
These are private words addressed to you in
    public.

       T. S. Eliot, American, 1888–1965

Flowers in a Chinese Vase. Odilon Redon, French,
1840–1916. Oil on canvas, before 1906.

[131]

The Lovers. Hishikawa Moronobu, Japanese, ca. 1625–
1694. Woodblock print, sumi-e, from a set of twelve sheets.

NOW SLEEPS THE CRIMSON
PETAL, NOW THE WHITE

Now sleeps the crimson petal, now the white;
Nor waves the cypress in the palace walk;
Nor winks the gold fin in the porphyry font.
The fire-fly wakens; waken thou with me.

Now droops the milk-white peacock like a ghost,
And like a ghost she glimmers on to me.

Now lies the Earth all Danaë to the stars,
And all thy heart lies open unto me.

Now slides the silent meteor on, and leaves
A shining furrow, as thy thoughts in me.

Now folds the lily all her sweetness up,
And slips into the bosom of the lake:
So fold thyself, my dearest, thou, and slip
Into my bosom and be lost in me.

ALFRED, LORD TENNYSON, English, 1809–1892

AMOROUS ANTICIPATION

Not the intimacy of your forehead clear as a
    celebration
nor the prize of your body, still mysterious and
    tacit and childlike
nor the sequence of your life showing itself in
    words or silence

will be so mysterious a favor
as to watch your dream implied
in the vigil of my arms.
Miraculously virgin again through the absolving
    virtue of sleep,
quiet and resplendent like a lucky choice of
    memories,
you will give me those far reaches of your life that
    you yourself do not have.

Cast into stillness,
I will perceive that ultimate strand of your being
and will see you for the first time, perhaps
as God must see you,
the fiction of Time destroyed,
without love, without me.

JORGE LUIS BORGES, Argentine, 1899–1986

The Bridal Chamber of Herse. Flemish (Brussels),
ca. 1550. Tapestry: wool, silk, silver, and silver-gilt thread.

PORTRAIT OF A WOMAN AT HER BATH

it is a satisfaction
a joy
to have one of those
in the house

when she takes a bath
she unclothes
herself she is no
Venus

I laugh at her
an Inca
shivering at the well
the sun is

glad of a fellow to
marvel at
the birds and the flowers
look in

WILLIAM CARLOS WILLIAMS, American,
1883–1963

The Bather.
Edgar Degas,
French, 1834–1917.
Pastel on paper,
ca. 1890.

THE GARRET

Come, let us pity those who are better off than we
    are.
Come, my friend, and remember
    that the rich have butlers and no friends,
And we have friends and no butlers.
Come, let us pity the married and the unmarried.

Dawn enters with little feet
    like a gilded Pavlova,
And I am near my desire.
Nor has life in it aught better
Than this hour of clear coolness,
    the hour of waking together.

EZRA POUND, American, 1885–1972

Ice Floes. Claude Monet, French, 1840–1926. Oil on canvas, 1893.

LOVE RECOGNIZED

There are many things in the world and you
Are one of them. Many things keep happening
    and
You are one of them, and the happening that
Is you keeps falling like snow
On the landscape of not-you, hiding hideousness,
    until
The streets and the world of wrath are choked
    with snow.

How many things have become silent? Traffic
Is throttled. The mayor
Has been, clearly, remiss, and the city
Was totally unprepared for such a crisis. Nor
    Was I—yes, why should this happen to me?
I have always been a law-abiding citizen.

But you, like snow, like love, keep falling,

And it is not certain that the world will not be
Covered in a glitter of crystalline whiteness.

Silence.

ROBERT PENN WARREN, American, 1905–1989

NATURAL HISTORY

(A letter to Katharine, from the King
Edward Hotel, Toronto)

The spider, dropping down from twig,
Unwinds a thread of her devising:
A thin, premeditated rig
To use in rising.

And all the journey down through space,
In cool descent, and loyal-hearted,
She builds a ladder to the place
From which she started.

Thus I, gone forth, as spiders do,
In spider's web a truth discerning,
Attach one silken strand to you
For my returning.

E. B. WHITE, American, 1899–1985

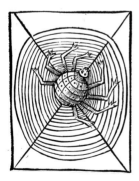

Spider. Woodcut
from *Hortus
sanitatis.*
Published in
Strasbourg by
Johann Prüss,
ca. 1497.

Painting. Joan Miró, Spanish, 1893–1983. Tempera and oil
on canvas, 1927.

FALL OF THE EVENING STAR

Speak softly; sun going down
Out of sight. Come near me now.

Dear dying fall of wings as birds
Complain against the gathering dark . . .

Exaggerate the green blood in grass;
The music of leaves scraping space;

Multiply the stillness by one sound;
By one syllable of your name . . .

And all that is little is soon giant,
All that is rare grows in common beauty

To rest with my mouth on your mouth
As somewhere a stars falls

And the earth takes it softly, in natural love . . .
Exactly as we take each other . . . and go to sleep.

KENNETH PATCHEN, American, 1911–1972

LOVE

So, the year's done with!
    (*Love me for ever!*)
All March begun with,
    April's endeavour;
May-wreaths that bound me
    June needs must sever;
Now snows fall round me,
Quenching June's fever—
    (*Love me for ever!*)

      ROBERT BROWNING, English, 1812–1889

SUCH DIFFERENT WANTS

The board floats on the river.
The board wants nothing
but is pulled from beneath
on into deeper waters.

And the elephant dwelling
on the mountain wants
a trumpet so its dying cry
can be heard by the stars.

The wakeful heron striding
through reeds at dawn wants
the god of sun and moon
to see his long skinny neck.

You must say what you want.
I want to be the man
and I am who will love you
when your hair is white.

      ROBERT BLY,
      American, b. 1926

Boating. Edouard Manet, French, 1832–1883. Oil on canvas, 1874.

FOR THE MOMENT

Life is simple and gay
The bright sun rings with a quiet sound
The sound of the bells has quieted down
This morning the light hits it all
The footlights of my head are lit again
And the room I live in is finally bright

Just one beam is enough
Just one burst of laughter
My joy that shakes the house
Restrains those wanting to die
By the notes of its song

I sing off-key
Ah it's funny
My mouth open to every breeze
Spews mad notes everywhere
That emerge I don't know how
To fly toward other ears

Listen I'm not crazy
I laugh at the bottom of the stairs
Before the wide-open door
In the sunlight scattered
On the wall among green vines
And my arms are held out toward you

It's today I love you

      PIERRE REVERDY, French, 1889–1960

The Swing. Hubert Robert, French, 1733–1808.
Oil on canvas.

THE DOUBLE BUBBLE
OF INFINITY

The night before the day of our wedding
I dreamed that the universe had a party,
All the stars were invited,
Beneath sparkling chandeliers, the planets
    rejoiced;

In all its beautiful, candle-lit galaxies,
Crowded with glass-clinking revellers,
The Cosmos was Laughing with
Lasting Love and Light.

KATE FARRELL, American, b. 1946

Landscape with Stars. Henri Edmond Cross, French, 1856–1910. Watercolor on paper.

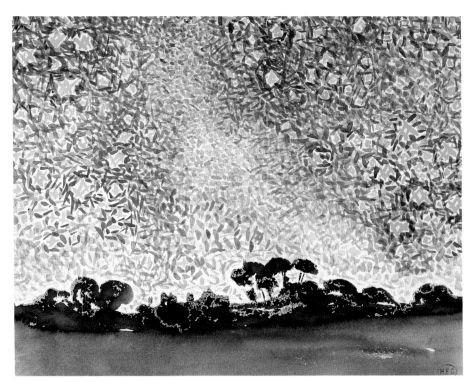

Fragmentary Head of a Queen.
Egyptian, ca. 1417–1379 B.C.,
Dynasty 18. Yellow jasper.

Soho Bedroom. Bill Brandt,
British, 1904–1983.
Gelatin silver print, 1936.

THE OLD WORDS

This is hard to say
Simply, because the words
Have grown so old together:
Lips and *eyes* and *tears,*
Touch and *fingers*
And *love,* out of love's language,
Are hard and smooth as stones
Laid bare in a streambed,
Not failing or fading
Like the halting speech of the body
Which will turn too suddenly
To ominous silence,
But like your lips and mine
Slow to separate, our fingers
Reluctant to come apart,
Our eyes and their slow tears
Reviving like these words
Springing to life again
And again, taken to heart,
To touch, love, to begin.

DAVID WAGONER, American, b. 1926

OLD SONG

Take off your clothes, love,
And come to me.

Soon will the sun be breaking
Over yon sea.

And all of our hairs be white, love,
For aught we do

And all our nights be one, love,
For all we knew.

ROBERT CREELEY, American, b. 1926

UNENDING LOVE

I seem to have loved you in numberless forms,
    numberless times,
In life after life, in age after age forever.
My spell-bound heart has made and re-made the
    necklace of songs
That you take as a gift, wear round your neck in
    your many forms
In life after life, in age after age forever.

Whenever I hear old chronicles of love, its age-old
    pain,
Its ancient tale of being apart or together,
As I stare on and on into the past, in the end you
    emerge
Clad in the light of a pole-star piercing the
    darkness of time:
You become an image of what is remembered
    forever.

You and I have floated here on the stream that
    brings from the fount
At the heart of time love of one for another.
We have played alongside millions of lovers, shared
    in the same
Shy sweetness of meeting, the same distressful
    tears of farewell—
Old love, but in shapes that renew and renew
    forever.

Today it is heaped at your feet, it has found its
    end in you,
The love of all man's days both past and forever:
Universal joy, universal sorrow, universal life,
The memories of all loves merging with this one
    love of ours—
And the songs of every poet past and forever.

       RABINDRANATH TAGORE, Indian, 1861-1941

Courtly Lovers. Signed by Reza-ye Abbasi, Iranian
(Safavid), Isfahan. Opaque watercolor, ink, and gold on paper,
dated 1039 A.H./A.D. 1630.

Give All
to Love

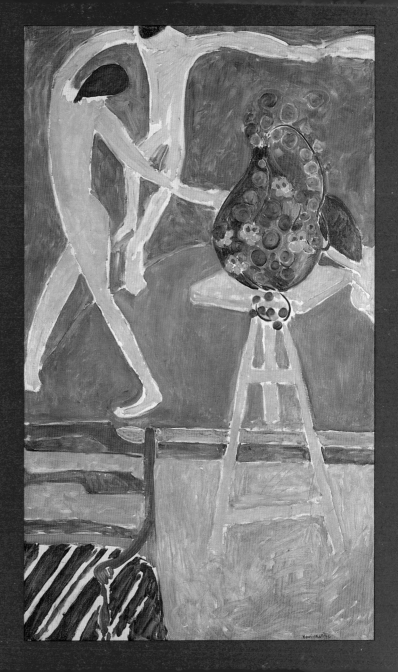

GIVE ALL TO LOVE

Give all to love;
Obey thy heart;
Friends, kindred, days,
Estate, good fame,
Plans, credit, and the Muse,—
Nothing refuse.

'Tis a brave master;
Let it have scope:
Follow it utterly,
Hope beyond hope:
High and more high
It dives into noon,
With wing unspent,
Untold intent;
But it is god,
Knows its own path
And the outlets of the sky.

It was never for the mean;
It requireth courage stout.
Souls above doubt,
Valor unbending,
It will reward,—
They shall return
More than they were,
And ever ascending.

Leave all for love;
Yet, hear me, yet,
One word more thy heart behoved,
One pulse more of firm endeavor,—
Keep thee today,
Tomorrow, forever,
Free as an Arab
Of thy beloved.

Cling with life to the maid;
But when the surprise,
First vague shadow of surmise
Flits across her bosom young,
Of a joy apart from thee,
Free be she, fancy free;
Nor thou detain her vesture's hem,
Nor the palest rose she flung
From her summer diadem.

Though thou loved her as thyself,
As a self of purer clay,
Though her parting dims the day,
Stealing grace from all alive;
Heartily know,
When half gods go,
The gods arrive.

RALPH WALDO EMERSON, American, 1803–1882

The Garden of Love. Peter
Paul Rubens, Flemish, 1577–
1640. Pen and brown ink and
colored washes.

Venus and the Lute Player. Titian (Tiziano Vecellio),
Italian (Venetian), ca. 1488–1576. Oil on canvas.

DARLING OF GOD AND MEN

FROM ON THE NATURE OF THINGS

Darling of God and Men, beneath the gliding
    stars
you fill rich earth and buoyant sea with your
    presence
for every living thing achieves its life through you,
rises and sees the sun. For you the sky is clear,
the tempest still. Deft earth scatters her gentle
    flowers,
the level ocean laughs, the softened heavens glow
with generous light for you. In the first days of
    spring
when the untrammelled all-renewing southwind
    blows
the birds exult in you and herald your coming.
Then the shy cattle leap and swim the brooks for
    love.
Everywhere, through all seas, mountains and
    waterfalls,
love caresses all hearts and kindles all creatures
to overmastering lust and ordained renewals.
Therefore, since you alone control the sum of
    things
and nothing without you comes forth into the
    light
and nothing beautiful or glorious can be
without you, Alma Venus! trim my poetry
with your grace: and give peace to write and read
    and think.

LUCRETIUS, Roman, ca. 99–55

SONG

Love and harmony combine,
And around our souls intwine,
While thy branches mix with mine,
And our roots together join.

Joys upon our branches sit,
Chirping loud, and singing sweet;
Like gentle streams beneath our feet
Innocence and virtue meet.

Thou the golden fruit dost bear,
I am clad in flowers fair;
Thy sweet boughs perfume the air,
And the turtle buildeth there.

There she sits and feeds her young,
Sweet I hear her mournful song;
And thy lovely leaves among,
There is love: I hear his tongue.

There his charming nest doth lay,
There he sleeps the night away;
There he sports along the day,
And doth among our branches play.

WILLIAM BLAKE, English, 1757–1827

Coverlet. Ann Walgrave Warner, American, made for
Phebe Warner. Linen and cotton, ca. 1800.

ANSWER TO A CHILD'S QUESTION

Do you ask what the birds say? The Sparrow, the
    Dove,
The Linnet and Thrush say, "I love and I love!"
In the winter they're silent—the wind is so
    strong;
What it says, I don't know, but it sings a loud
    song.
But green leaves, and blossoms, and sunny warm
    weather,
And singing, and loving—all come back together.
But the Lark is so brimful of gladness and love,
The green fields below him, the blue sky above,
That he sings, and he sings; and for ever sings
    he—
"I love my Love, and my Love loves me!"

              SAMUEL TAYLOR COLERIDGE, English, 1772–1834

Peaceable Kingdom. Edward Hicks, American,
1780–1849. Oil on canvas, ca. 1830.

WHAT THERE IS

In this my green world
Flowers birds are hands
They hold me
I am loved all day

All this pleases me

I am amused
I have to laugh from crying
Trees mountains are arms
I am loved all day

Children grass are tears

I cry
I am loved all day
Everything
Pompous makes me laugh
I am amused often enough
In this
My beautiful green world

There's love all day

              KENNETH PATCHEN,
              American, 1911–1972

ISAIAH 1t Chap. 6 & 6

LOVE POEM

Yours is the face that the earth turns to me.
Continuous beyond its human features lie
The mountain forms that rest against the sky.
With your eyes, the reflecting rainbow, the sun's
    light
Sees me; forest and flowers, bird and beast
Know and hold me forever in the world's thought,
Creation's deep untroubled retrospect.

When your hand touches mine, it is the earth
That takes me—the deep grass,
And rocks and rivers; the green graves,
And children still unborn, and ancestors,
In love passed down from hand to hand from God.
Your love comes from the creation of the world,
From those paternal fingers, streaming through
    the clouds
That break with light the surface of the sea.

Here, where I trace your body with my hand,
Love's presence has no end;
For these, your arms that hold me, are the world's.
In us, the continents, clouds and oceans meet
Our arbitrary selves, extensive with the night,
Lost, in the heart's worship, and the body's sleep.

      KATHLEEN RAINE, English, b. 1908

The Heart of the Andes. Frederic Edwin Church,
American, 1826–1900. Oil on canvas, 1859.

IN LOVE FOR LONG

I've been in love for long
With what I cannot tell
And will contrive a song
For the intangible
That has no mould or shape,
From which there's no escape.

It is not even a name,
Yet is all constancy;
Tried or untried, the same,
It cannot part from me;
A breath, yet as still
As the established hill.

It is not anything,
And yet all being is;
Being, being, being,
Its burden and its bliss.
How can I ever prove
What it is I love?

This happy happy love
Is sieged with crying sorrows,
Crushed beneath and above
Between todays and morrows;
A little paradise
Held in the world's vice.

And there it is content
And careless as a child,
And in imprisonment
Flourishes sweet and wild;
In wrong, beyond wrong,
All the world's day long.

This love a moment known
For what I do not know
And in a moment gone
Is like the happy doe
That keeps its perfect laws
Between the tiger's paws
And vindicates its cause.

EDWIN MUIR, Scottish, 1887–1959

Improvisation Number 27: The Garden of Love.
Wassily Kandinsky, Russian, 1866–1944. Oil on canvas,
1912.

THE WOMAN IN SUNSHINE

It is only that this warmth and movement are like
The warmth and movement of a woman.

It is not that there is any image in the air
Nor the beginning nor end of a form:

It is empty. But a woman in threadless gold
Burns us with brushings of her dress

And a dissociated abundance of being,
More definite for what she is—

Because she is disembodied,
Bearing the odors of the summer fields,

Confessing the taciturn and yet indifferent,
Invisibly clear, the only love.

WALLACE STEVENS, American, 1879–1955

SOLO FOR SATURDAY
NIGHT GUITAR

Time was. Time is. Time shall be.
Man invented time to be used.
Love was. Love is. Love shall be.
Yet man never invented love
Nor is love to be used like time.
A clock wears numbers one to twelve
And you look and read its face
And tell the time pre-cise-ly ex-act-ly.
Yet who reads the face of love?
Who tells love numbers pre-cise-ly ex-act-ly?
Holding love in a tight hold for keeps,
Fastening love down and saying
"It's here now and here for always."
You don't do this offhand, careless-like.
Love costs. Love is not so easy
Nor is the shimmering of star dust

Nor the smooth flow of new blossoms
Nor the drag of a heavy hungering for someone.
   Love is a white horse you ride
   or wheels and hammers leaving you lonely
   or a rock in the moonlight for rest
   or a sea where phantom ships cross always
   or a tall shadow always whispering
   or a circle of spray and prisms—
   maybe a rainbow round your shoulder.
      Heavy heavy is love to carry
      and light as one rose petal,
      light as a bubble, a blossom,
      a remembering bar of music
      or a finger or a wisp of hair
      never forgotten.

CARL SANDBURG, American, 1878–1967

Love and Innocence Clock. French, ca. 1825. Gilt bronze.

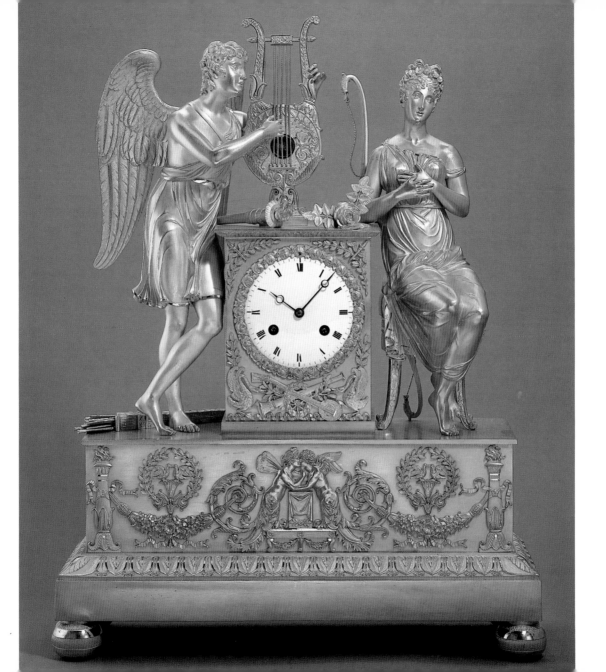

LOVE WHAT IT IS

Love is a circle that doth restless move
In the same sweet eternity of love.

ROBERT HERRICK, English, 1591–1674

Les Attitudes sont faciles et chastes. Maurice Denis, French, 1870–1943. Color lithograph, ca. 1899, from the suite *Amour*.

LOVE LIVES BEYOND THE TOMB

Love lives beyond
The tomb, the earth, which fades like dew—
I love the fond,
The faithful, and the true.

Love lies in sleep,
The happiness of healthy dreams,
Eve's dews may weep,
But love delightful seems.

'Tis seen in flowers,
And in the even's pearly dew
On earth's green hours,
And in the heaven's eternal blue.

'Tis heard in spring
When light and sunbeams, warm and kind,
On angel's wing
Bring love and music to the wind.

And where is voice
So young, so beautiful, and sweet
As nature's choice,
Where spring and lovers meet?

Love lives beyond
The tomb, the earth, the flowers, and dew.
I love the fond,
The faithful, young, and true.

JOHN CLARE, English, 1793–1864

The Portico of a Country Mansion. Hubert Robert,
French, 1733–1808. Oil on canvas.

LINES

To a Movement in Mozart's E-Flat Symphony

    Show me again the time
      When in the Junetide's prime
  We flew by meads and mountains northerly!—
Yea, to such freshness, fairness, fulness, fineness,
    freeness,
      Love lures life on.

    Show me again the day
      When from the sandy bay
  We looked together upon the pestered sea!—
Yea, to such surging, swaying, sighing, swelling,
    shrinking,
      Love lures life on.

    Show me again the hour
      When by the pinnacled tower
  We eyed each other and feared futurity!—
Yea, to such bodings, broodings, beatings,
    blanchings, blessings,
      Love lures life on.

    Show me again just this:
      The moment of that kiss
  Away from the prancing folk, by the
    strawberry-tree!—
Yea, to such rashness, ratheness, rareness,
    ripeness, richness,
      Love lures life on.

      THOMAS HARDY, English, 1840–1928

BRIGHT STAR, WOULD I WERE STEDFAST AS THOU ART

Bright star, would I were stedfast as thou art—
    Not in lone splendor hung aloft the night,
And watching, with eternal lids apart,
    Like nature's patient, sleepless eremite,
The moving waters at their priestlike task
    Of pure ablution round earth's human shores,
Or gazing on the new soft-fallen mask
    Of snow upon the mountains and the moors;
No—yet still stedfast, still unchangeable,
    Pillow'd upon my fair love's ripening breast,
To feel for ever its soft swell and fall,
    Awake for ever in a sweet unrest,
Still, still to hear her tender-taken breath,
And so live ever—or else swoon to death.

      JOHN KEATS, English, 1795–1821

Dante and Beatrice with the Blessed Souls. Woodcut from *Comedia dell'Inferno, del Purgatorio, & del Paradiso*, Canto 27 of *Paradiso*, by Dante Alighieri. Venice: Published by Giovambattista and Melchiorre Sessa et Fratelli, 1578.

The Fly. William Blake, English, 1757–1827. Hand-colored relief etching, heightened with gold, from *Songs of Innocence and of Experience*, 1789–94 (printed in 1825).

LATE FRAGMENT

And did you get what
you wanted from this life, even so?
I did.
And what did you want?
To call myself beloved, to feel myself
beloved on the earth.

RAYMOND CARVER, American, 1938–1988

Akhenaton Holding an Olive Branch. Egyptian,
ca. 1373–1362 B.C., Dynasty 18. Painted limestone.

ONCE MORE, THE ROUND

What's greater, Pebble or Pond?
What can be known? The Unknown.
My true self runs toward a Hill
More! O More! visible.

Now I adore my life
With the Bird, the abiding Leaf,
With the Fish, the questing Snail,
And the Eye altering all;
And I dance with William Blake
For love, for Love's sake;

And everything comes to One,
As we dance on, dance on, dance on.

THEODORE ROETHKE, American, 1908–1963

THE WORLD WAS WARM AND WHITE WHEN I WAS BORN

The world was warm and white when I was born:
Beyond the windowpane the world was white,
A glaring whiteness in a leaded frame,
Yet warm as in the hearth and heart of light.
Although the whiteness was almond and was bone
In midnight's still paralysis, nevertheless
The world was warm and hope was infinite
All things would come, fulfilled, all things would
   be known
All things would be enjoyed, fulfilled, and come to
   be my own.

How like a summer the years of youth have
   passed!
—How like the summer of 1914, in all truth!—
Patience, my soul, the truth is never known
Until the future has become the past
And then, only, when the love of truth at last
Becomes the truth of love, when both are one,
Then, then, then, Eden becomes Utopia and is
   surpassed:
For then the dream of knowledge and knowledge
   knows
Motive and joy at once wherever it goes.

DELMORE SCHWARTZ, American, 1913–1966

The Visit to the Lying-in Chamber (detail). Gabriel Metsu, Dutch, 1629–1667. Oil on canvas, 1661.

LOVE TELLS US WHO WE ARE

Love Tells Us Who
We Are.
When I asked the
Answer "Who?"
No Love Answered
So I knew I
Had to Wait
For Love

For
We are No one
Before Love
A missing clue looking
For a Person
A Star looking for
A sky
An "I am" waiting for
An I

Music Tells Us
What We Feel
But Cannot Say
Love Reveals
What We Know
But cannot See

Before You I was Nothing But
When You Gave me Your Hand
I took My Hand
For Love Tells Us Who
We Are So
When I asked the
Answer "Who?"
Love Answered
You.

DONALD T. SANDERS,
American, b. 1944

Paradise (detail). Giovanni di Paolo, Italian (Sienese), active by 1417, d. 1482. Tempera on canvas, transferred from wood; ca. 1445.

ACKNOWLEDGMENTS

Grateful acknowledgment is made to the following for permission to print the copyrighted material listed below.

Owen Barfield: "Sonnet" reprinted by permission of the author.

Elizabeth Barnett: "The Spring and the Fall" by Edna St. Vincent Millay. From *Collected Poems*, Harper & Row. Copyright 1923, 1951 by Edna St. Vincent Millay and Norma Millay Ellis. Reprinted by permission.

Willis Barnstone: "Lament" by Pindar, "Love Poem" by Plato, and "The Street in Shadow" by Antonio Machado Ruiz, translated by Willis Barnstone. Reprinted by permission of the translator.

Mary Ursula Bethell: "Response" reprinted by permission of the Trustees in the estate of the late Mary Ursula Bethell.

Black Sparrow Press: "wearing the collar" © 1986 by Charles Bukowski. Reprinted from *You get so alone at times it just makes sense* with permission of Black Sparrow Press.

Robert Bly: "After Drinking All Night With a Friend, We Go Out in a Boat at Dawn to See Who Can Write the Best Poem" by Robert Bly. Reprinted from *Silence in the Snowy Fields*, Wesleyan University Press, 1962, copyright © 1962 by Robert Bly. Reprinted by permission of the author. "Such Different Wants" reprinted by permission of the author and Doubleday.

Broadside Press: "Souvenirs" by Dudley Randall reprinted from *Counterpoem* by permission of Broadside Press, Detroit, Michigan.

Jonathan Cape Ltd.: "The Telephone" and "The Impulse" from *The Poetry of Robert Frost*, edited by Edward Connery Lathem, reprinted by permission of the Estate of Robert Frost, the editor, and Jonathan Cape Ltd.

Carcanet Press Limited: "Chance" by H. D. (Hilda Doolittle) from *Collected Poems 1912–1944*. Reprinted by permission of Carca- net Press Limited. "Love Song," "Portrait of a Lady," and "Portrait of a Woman at Her Bath" by William Carlos Williams from *Collected Poems*, volumes I and II. Reprinted by permission of Carcanet Press Limited.

City Lights: "Bars" by Nicolás Guillén, "For Aitana" by Rafael Alberti, "Our Child" by Pablo Neruda, "Rocking My Child" by Gabriela Mistral, and "Amorous Anticipation" by Jorge Luis Borges from *Love Poems of Spain and Spanish America*, translated by Perry Higman. Copyright © 1986 by Perry Higman. Reprinted by permission of City Lights Books. "Crystal Palace Market" and "I Want to Breathe" by James Laughlin from *Selected Poems*. Copyright © 1986 by James Laughlin. Reprinted by permission of City Lights Books. "Variation" by Federico García Lorca from *Ode to Walt Whitman & Other Poems*, translated by Carlos Bauer. Copyright © 1988 by Carlos Bauer. Reprinted by permission of City Lights Books.

Collins Publishers: "Joys That Sting" by C. S. Lewis from *Poems*. Reprinted by permission of Collins Publishers, London. "somewhere i have never travelled,gladly beyond" and "your birthday comes to tell me this" by e.e. cummings from *Complete Poems 1913–1962*. Reprinted by permission of Grafton Books, a division of William Collins Sons & Co. Ltd.

Constable Publishers: "Children," "Oath of Friendship" and "The Rejected Wife" from *170 Chinese Poems*, translated by Arthur Waley. Reprinted by permission of Constable Publishers.

Curtis Brown, Ltd.: "My Woman" by Catullus, from *Poets in a Landscape*, translated by Gilbert Highet. Reprinted by permission of Curtis Brown, Ltd. Copyright © 1957 by Gilbert Highet.

Devin-Adair, Publishers: Copyright by Devin-Adair, Publishers, Inc., Old Greenwich, Connecticut, 06870. Permission granted to reprint "In Memory of My Mother" from *The Collected Poems* by Patrick Kavanagh, 1964. All rights reserved.

printed by permission of Harcourt Brace Jovanovich, Inc. "Solo for Saturday Night Guitar" from *Honey and Salt*, copyright © 1963 by Carl Sandburg, reprinted by permission of Harcourt Brace Jovanovich, Inc. "Parting" from *Happy as a Dog's Tale*, copyright © 1980 by Anna Swirszczynska, reprinted by permission of Harcourt Brace Jovanovich, Inc.

Harper & Row, Publishers, Inc.: "I Walked Past A House Where I Lived Once" and "A Child Is Something Else Again" from *The Selected Poetry of Yehuda Amichai*, edited and translated by Chana Bloch and Stephen Mitchell. English translation copyright © 1986 by Chana Bloch and Stephen Mitchell. Reprinted by permission of Harper & Row, Publishers, Inc. "Past One O'Clock..." from *The Bedbug and Selected Poetry* by Vladimir Mayakovsky. Copyright © 1960 by the World Publishing Co. Reprinted by permission of Harper & Row, Publishers, Inc. "Natural History" from *Poems and Sketches of E. B. White*. Copyright 1929 by E. B. White. Reprinted by permission of Harper & Row, Publishers, Inc.

Henry Holt and Company, Inc.: "The Telephone" and "The Impulse" by Robert Frost. Copyright 1916 by Holt, Rinehart and Winston, Inc. and renewed 1944 by Robert Frost. Reprinted from *The Poetry of Robert Frost* edited by Edward Connery Lathem, by permission of Henry Holt and Company, Inc. "When I Was One-and-Twenty." Copyright 1939, 1940, © 1965 by Holt, Rinehart and Winston, Inc. Copyright © 1967, 1968 by Robert E. Symons. Reprinted from *The Collected Poems of A. E. Housman*, by permission of Henry Holt and Company, Inc.

Olwyn Hughes: "Yesterday He Still Looked in My Eyes" and "Where Does This Tenderness Come From?" from *Selected Poems of Marina Tsvetayeva*. Copyright © 1971. Reprinted by permission of Olwyn Hughes.

Indiana University Press: "I Can't Hold You and I Can't Leave You" by Sor Juana Inés DeLa Cruz from *Anthology of Mexican Poetry*. Edited by Octavio Paz, translated by Samuel Beckett, published by Indiana University Press.

International Creative Management, Inc.: "Energy" and "Late Fragment." Reprinted by permission of Tess Gallagher for The Estate of Raymond Carver. Copyright © 1985 by Raymond Carver. From *Where Water Comes Together With Other Water*, published by Random House, 1985.

John Johnson Limited: "She's Gazing at You So Tenderly" by Alexander Pushkin. Translation © D. M. Thomas, from *The Bronze Horseman*, The Viking Press, 1982.

Jane Kenyon: "Everything Promised Him To Me." This poem first appeared in *Twenty Poems of Anna Akhmatova*, translated by Jane Kenyon and Vera Dunham; The Eighties/Ally Press; St. Paul, Mn.

Kenneth Koch: "To You" copyright © 1962, 1985 by the author. "Sonnet" by Dante Alighieri, translated by Kenneth Koch. Copyright © 1973, 1986 by Kenneth Koch.

Liveright: "somewhere i have never travelled,gladly beyond" is reprinted from *Viva, poems by E. E. Cummings*, Edited by George James Firmage, by permission of Liveright Publishing Corporation. Copyright 1931, 1959 by E. E. Cummings. Copyright © 1979, 1973 by the Trustees for the E. E. Cummings Trust. Copyright © 1979, 1973 by George James Firmage. "your birthday comes to tell me this" is reprinted from *Complete Poems, 1913–1962*, by E. E. Cummings, by permission of Liveright Publishing Corporation. Copyright © 1923, 1925, 1931, 1935, 1938, 1939, 1940, 1944, 1945, 1946, 1947, 1948, 1949, 1950, 1951, 1952, 1953, 1954, 1955, 1956, 1957, 1958, 1959, 1960, 1961, 1962 by the Trustees for the E. E. Cummings Trust. Copyright © 1961, 1963, 1968 by Marion Morehouse Cummings.

Macmillan Publishing Company: "Lines to a Movement in Mozart's E-Flat Symphony" by Thomas Hardy. From *The Complete Poems of Thomas Hardy*, edited by James Gibson (New York: Macmillan, 1978). "I Have Loved Hours at Sea" by Sara Teasdale. Reprinted with permission of Macmillan Publishing Company from *Collected Poems* by Sara Teasdale. Copyright 1920 by Macmillan Publishing Company, renewed 1943 by Mamie T. Wheless. "A Drinking Song," "He Wishes for the Cloths of Heaven," and "When You Are Old" by W. B. Yeats. From *The Poems of W. B. Yeats: A New Edition*, edited by Richard J. Finneran (New York: Macmillan, 1983).

CREDITS

My-ness

Page 13: Gift of Mr. and Mrs. Charles Wrightsman, 1981   1981.238
Page 14: Gift of Edgar William and Bernice Chrysler Garbisch, 1966   66.242.3
Page 15: Amelia B. Lazarus Fund, by exchange, 1917   13.90
Page 16: Rogers Fund, 1922   JP 1278
Page 17: The Friedsam Collection. Bequest of Michael Friedsam, 1931   32.100.5
Page 18: Gift of George N. and Helen M. Richard, 1964   64.165.2
Page 20: Gift of Albert Weatherby, 1946   46.17
Page 21: The Jules Bache Collection, 1949   49.7.41
Page 22: Rogers Fund, 1946   46.43.1
Page 23: Catharine Lorillard Wolfe Collection, Bequest of Catharine Lorillard Wolfe, 1887   87.15.22
Page 24: The Mr. and Mrs. Henry Ittleson, Jr. Purchase Fund, 1956   56.13
Page 25: Robert Lehman Collection, 1975   1975.1.225
Page 26: Bequest of Benjamin Altman, 1913   14.40.619
Page 28: Gift of Lila Acheson Wallace, 1983   1983.1009 (8)

Oath of Friendship

Page 29: Bequest of Sam A. Lewisohn, 1951   51.112.4
Page 31: Gift of Julia A. Berwind, 1953   53.225.4
Page 32: Wentworth Fund, 1949   49.24
Page 33: Samuel D. Lee Fund, 1939   39.14
Pages 34–35: Gift of The Dillon Fund, 1973   1973.120.6
Page 36: Alfred Stieglitz Collection, 1933   33.43.74
Page 37: The Friedsam Collection. Bequest of Michael Friedsam, 1931   32.100.21
Page 38: Bequest of Maria DeWitt Jesup, from the collection of her husband, Morris K. Jesup, 1914   15.30.61
Page 39: Purchase, Mrs. Arthur Hays Sulzberger Gift, 1972   1972.128
Page 40: Gift of friends of John Sloan, 1928   28.18

Page 42: Bequest of Amelia B. Lazarus, 1906   07.88.4
Page 43: Rogers Fund, 1949   49.30
Page 44: Gift of Mrs. Russell Sage, 1908   08.228

Go, Lovely Rose

Page 45: The Jules Bache Collection, 1949   49.7.49
Page 46: Rogers Fund, 1925   25.181
Page 47: Catharine Lorillard Wolfe Collection, Bequest of Catharine Lorillard Wolfe, 1887   87.15.134
Page 48: Gift of Mrs. J. Insley Blair, 1950   50.228.3
Page 49: Gift of Mrs. Elliott L. Kamen, in memory of her father, Bernard R. Armour, 1960   60.122
Page 50: Gift of Louis C. Raegner, 1927   27.200
Page 51: Gift of Thomas F. Ryan, 1913   13.164.2
Page 52: Purchase, The Martin S. Ackerman Foundation Gift, 1979   1979.184
Page 53: Marquand Collection, Gift of Henry G. Marquand, 1889   89.15.19
Page 55: Gift of Jessie Woolworth Donahue, 1956   56.100.1
Page 56: The Jules Bache Collection, 1949   49.7.46
Page 57: Gift of Katrin S. Vietor, in loving memory of Ernest G. Vietor, 1966   66.36
Pages 58–59: Rogers Fund, 1929   29.23.1
Page 60: Bequest of Miss Adelaide Milton de Groot (1876–1967), 1967   67.187.141
Page 61: Bequest of William Church Osborn, 1951   51.30.2
Page 62: Rogers Fund, 1922   JP 1327
Page 63: Bequest of Miss Adelaide Milton de Groot (1876–1967), 1967   67.187.121
Page 64: Anonymous Gift, 1986   1986.404
Page 65: The Jack and Belle Linsky Collection, 1982   1982.60.191–192
Page 66: Gift of Mr. and Mrs. Samuel Shore, 1978   1978.61.4–6

Let Me Count The Ways

Page 67: Purchased with special contributions and purchase funds given or bequeathed by friends of the Museum, 1967   67.241

Page 68: Gift of Irwin Untermyer, 1964   64.101.519
Page 69: Bequest of William K. Vanderbilt, 1920   20.155.9
Page 70: Marquand Fund, 1959   59.120
Page 71: Rogers Fund, 1906   06.1322.2
Page 72: Bequest of William Church Osborn, 1951   51.30.4
Page 73: George A. Hearn Fund, 1907   07.140
Page 74: Gift of Julia A. Berwind, 1953   53.225.7
Page 75: Bequest of Edward S. Harkness, 1940   50.135.5
Page 76: Bequest of Stephen C. Clark, 1960   61.101.14
Page 77: Fletcher Fund, 1958   58.89
Page 78: Gift of Lila Acheson Wallace, 1983   1983.1009 (7)
Page 79: Wolfe Fund, Catharine Lorillard Wolfe Collection, 1952   52.183
Page 80: George A. Hearn Fund, 1966   66.171
Page 81: Bequest of Mrs. H. O. Havemeyer, 1929, H. O. Havemeyer Collection   29.100.110
Page 82: Purchase, Lila Acheson Wallace Gift, Arthur Hoppock Hearn Fund, Arthur Lejwa Fund in honor of Jean Arp; and The Bernhill Fund, Joseph H. Hazen Foundation, Inc., Samuel I. Newhouse Foundation, Inc., Walter Bareiss, Marie Bannon McHenry, Louise Smith and Stephen C. Swid Gifts, 1980   1980.420
Page 83: The Evelyn Sharp Collection, New York. Courtesy of The Evelyn Sharp Collection
Page 84: Bequest of Benjamin Altman, 1913   14.40.622

The Mess of Love

Page 85: Bequest of Mrs. H. O. Havemeyer, 1929, H. O. Havemeyer Collection   29.100.43
Page 86: Ford Motor Company Collection, Gift of Ford Motor Company and John C. Waddell, 1987   1987.1100.7
Page 87: Munsey Fund, 1934   34.138
Page 88: Purchase, Joseph Pulitzer Bequest, 1921   21.116
Page 89: Rogers Fund, 1903   03.14.13
Page 90: Warner Communications Inc. Purchase Fund, 1980   1980.1023.5

Yesterday He Still Looked in My Eyes

The Marriage of True Minds

Give All to Love

INDEX OF ARTISTS

INDEX OF AUTHORS AND TITLES

INDEX OF FIRST LINES

[174]

[175]